WELCOME

TO

A

HEALTHY

ALTERNATIVE

BY

SUSAN CALDER

FRONT COVER:
LANCASHIRE HOT POT (BEEF STEW) P. 59

WELCOME TO A HEALTHY ALTERNATIVE

BY: SUSAN CALDER

1ST PRINTING JULY 1993

COPYRIGHT © 1993 BY:

SUSAN CALDER
1534 SHORNCLIFFE HEIGHTS
VICTORIA, B.C. CANADA V8P 5R6

CANADIAN CATALOGUING IN PUBLICATION DATA

CALDER, SUSAN
     WELCOME TO A HEALTHY ALTERNATIVE

INCLUDES INDEX
ISBN 0-895292-25-5

1. MICROWAVE COOKERY   2. COOKERY FOR ONE

3. COOKERY FOR TWO   4. LOW-CALORIE DIET-RECIPES

5. LOW-CHOLESTEROL DIET-RECIPES 6. SALT-FREE DIET-RECIPES

I. TITLE
TX 832. C353 1993   641.5'6   C93-098134-0

PHOTOGRAPHY BY: STIRLING WARD PHOTOGRAPHIC DESIGN
                 VANCOUVER, B.C.

HAND LETTERED BY: HEATHER HAINES

TIP DESIGN BY: ROBIN PEARSON

DESIGNED, PRINTED & PRODUCED IN CANADA BY:
     PRINTWEST LTD.

PUBLISHING CONSULTANT & FOOD STYLIST:
     MARGO EMBURY
     1150 EIGHTH AVENUE
     REGINA, SASKATCHEWAN
     CANADA S4R 1C9
     (306) 525-2304
       FAX : 757-2439

TABLE OF CONTENTS

This book is dedicated to my husband Doug & children Debbie, Kim, Allison & David....
I am most thankful for their patience and willingness to be guinea pigs!

A special thanks to family & close friends whose confidence & support has helped me to "press on".

A big "thank you" to those cheery personalities who attend my cooking classes; "you make my day!"

I also thank Diane Blaney, RDN, of Quilchena Consulting Ltd. (See P. 125) for the nutrient analysis of the recipes, and Darlene Ravensdale, RDN, for her suggestions.

Another special "thank you" to Val Spears for her expertise in proof reading.

And last but not least, to my buddy Heather, who not only hand printed the book but edited it with a fine-toothed comb until it was perfect!

INTRODUCTION

A HEALTHY ALTERNATIVE:
MICROWAVING FOR ONE OR TWO

SHELVES & DRAWERS FULL OF RECIPES?

I have found in my travels that most people who are cooking for one or two have tons of recipes! It is a bother & not energy efficient to turn on a large range & also when I'm cooking for one or two I really don't want to do a recipe that is complicated or has too many ingredients. I've designed this book as a tool to assist you in doing your own recipes in the microwave oven & have given you some new ones, keeping in mind the rules for healthy eating.

RULES FOR HEALTHY EATING:

Follow the NEW Canada Food Guide, include lots of whole grains & vegetables, cut back on fat & where possible eliminate any animal fat. Salt is also something to consider cutting back on. In the microwave oven food cooks in less time so a lot of the flavor is retained. This will eliminate the need to add salt. Added fat is not re-quired to grease pans, sauté vegetables or for pan frying. All of this can be done without the fat because there is no dry air in the microwave oven & no direct heat to make foods stick to the dish. If you are sauteing vegetables without fat, just put a lid on the dish to keep the moisture in.

GENERAL RULES:
REGULAR OVEN VERSUS MICROWAVE OVEN

It is often said that microwaving is so different from cooking with a "regular oven", & in some ways it is. Microwave ovens produce moist heat as compared to the dry heat of a regular oven ..... of course cooking times are much shorter. However, there are many similarities & the following ideas will help you with your microwave cooking:

"REGULAR" OVEN Foods that cook:	MICROWAVE OVEN Will cook:
· on high heat (elements)	· on high heat (full power)
· on slow cook	· on medium or medium low
· uncovered	· uncovered or wax paper
· with a lid or foil	· with a lid or plastic wrap
· stir or rearrange	· stir or rearrange
· in a shallow dish	· in a shallow dish
· in a roasting pan	· in a microwave-safe roasting pan

Follow the same rules for determining if the food is cooked before standing time: (eg) the fish will flake, juices run clear on the poultry & meat has lost its pink colour. Vegetables, however will still be a little tender-crisp & will soften on standing.

- Foods that steam cook ... cover with a lid or plastic wrap.
- Foods that bake or roast ... cook uncovered or with a loose tent of wax paper.
- Foods high in bacteria (eg) chicken, ground beef etc..... should be cooked with a lid or wax paper.
- Foods that slow cook (eg) soups or stews, will take ⅓ of the time in the microwave (45 minutes - 1 hour). If you want you can start on high to build up the heat & then turn the power down to medium or medium low to slow cook or to prevent it from boiling over.
- Anything that you would cook on top of the stove can be done in the microwave oven. As there is no direct heat, this is a superior method for most foods... however... I have to confess that large quantities of water will boil faster in a kettle or on top of the stove.
- Dishes going into the microwave oven do not need greasing unless you are following a recipe that states to do so.

MICROWAVABLE PRODUCTS:

DISHES: The microwave energy passes through everything except metal.... but steam & the heat of the fats & sug-

INTRODUCTION

ars will burn your skin. Therefore, you shouldn't use metal dishes, & the other dishes you do use must be able to tolerate the high heat. For this reason, margarine containers & some plastic wraps are NOT microwave safe. In the line of plastics you use, make sure they are labelled "microwave safe". An excellent product on the market is "micro mac". This is a Canadian-made line of plasticware that is very popular because it can tolerate the heat of the foods, it is light & easy to handle which is important for children or arthritic fingers .... & best of all it does not stain as do other microwave plastics. All Corning & Pyrex, etc.... are great. Clay bakers work well as do the liners for a lot of the crock pots.

ROASTING PAN: When you buy a "regular oven", they give you roasting pans because the manufacturer knows that if you don't use this kind of pan, you can't roast properly. You know that if you put a roast in a casserole in the regular oven, you will steam it or "pot roast" it. For the same reason, it is important to elevate the meat out of its juices in the microwave oven. If you don't have a proper meat tray (bacon rack, hot dog cooker or whatever the manufacturers want to call them), you can use

an inverted saucer.... but if you put your meat
into a casserole, it will steam cook or stew.

CAKE PAN: cakes will bake better in
plastic than in glass pans. We know that glassware gets hot in the microwave oven, & the
only possible way it can get hot is by taking
some of the heat from the food. We therefore
find that in a glass pan, the cake will be tacky
or wet on all the sides where it is touching
the glass ... the glass has taken the heat that
that part of the cake needs to bake. Whenever
possible I use plastic cake pans. For small, one
layer cakes, an eight inch is fine, but for your
larger cake recipes a "Bundt" pan or ring mold
(these are doughnut-shaped) is preferable.
In most microwave ovens, all of the outside
edges of the food cook faster than the centre
and the Bundt pan allows the energy to come
in through the centre edges as well as the outside edges. This allows for even baking of a
cake.

BROWNING DISHES: these are not brown
dishes nor are they the same as roasting
pans that allow larger portions of meat to
brown. They are dishes that have a special
coating on the bottom that attracts energy
& they get hot in the microwave oven. They
then work as a skillet. They give you that
direct heat similar to what an element
would give for frying or searing foods. They

INTRODUCTION

are made of a microwaveable product so that you can cook right on them in the microwave oven.

   PLASTIC WRAPS: the only time you will need plastic wrap is when you don't have a lid for the dish or a dinner plate that will work as a lid. When you do use a plastic wrap, make sure it is labelled "microwave safe". Some of the wraps will not tolerate the heat of the steam or the food & will break down into things that you don't want to know about!

CONVERTING:

   It's better to follow microwave recipes at first. You'll soon get to know the timings & covers to use. When you're ready to start converting, find a microwave recipe that is similar & adjust the time & ingredients accordingly.

   CASSEROLES : you may want to pre-cook onions for casseroles, as sometimes the speed of cooking is so great, they don't get a chance to soften. You'll also find that because of the speed of cooking, there won't be as much evaporation of liquids .... (eg) a casserole full of cooked ingredients to serve 2-4 people, will take 3-6 minutes on full power.

INTRODUCTION

CAKES: when I do a cake or muffins from a recipe for the regular oven, I do the recipe as is but..... I use a medium size egg (instead of large) & I let the batter sit for 5 minutes before I bake it - (either in the pan or the batter bowl, it doesn't matter.) If I find the cake takes too long to bake off the moisture, I make a note to cut back the moisture by 25% the next time I bake it.

   8" (20cm) recipe: cook on high 4-7 minutes
   Bundt pan recipe: cook on high 8-14 minutes
   6 muffins: cook on high 2½ - 3½ minutes
 * Test with a cake tester (long toothpick)
 * See CAKES (P. 96-97).

COVERS TO USE:

Many people ask when to use plastic wrap & when to use wax paper. Use the following guide, thinking of the end product & what you want to achieve:

PLASTIC WRAP: some are better than others. Use those that are marked "microwave-safe", only. It works the same as a glass lid. Use it (or your microwave safe lid) whenever you're doing vegetables, poaching fish, pot roasting etc. Because plastic wrap forms such a tight seal, turn a corner back to allow a steam vent. (This works better than puncturing the top, as the slit often gets larger with steam pressure, you lose too much steam & in some cases, this will dry out your food).

* It's important to know that you never have to use plastic wrap if you have a lid, plate or something that will keep the steam in.

WAX PAPER: use wax paper when-ever you are roasting. This cover sits loosely on top of the food, & will allow a lot of the steam to escape. Use it for roast chicken (whole or pieces) & some casseroles. It also works well for foods high in bacteria (chicken, ground beef etc) that you don't want to steam with a lid. It keeps the heat to the food, but allows the steam to escape.

PAPER TOWEL: paper towel has two main uses .... whenever you are warming bread products, you should wrap them in paper towel. Bread products are very por-ous & heat very quickly. The moisture will evaporate & unless the bread is covered, the fan will send the moisture away. If you cover the bread with plastic wrap, the moisture will condense on the wrap & leave the bread product damp. However, paper towel absorbs the moisture & will leave the bread moist. The other use for paper towel is when cooking bacon .... the paper towel absorbs the fat & spatters.

ALUMINUM FOIL: aluminum foil is used for shielding. Remember radiowaves pass through everything except metal. If there is an area of your food that is over-cooking, such as the legs on a turkey or the thin area of an odd-shaped roast, just put a small amount of aluminum foil on that part. The radiowaves will then deflect off the foil & go to the area that needs more cooking. Some important rules of thumb when using foil are:

1) Don't cover more than ¼ of the mass; the majority of the food should be ex-posed.
2) Make sure the foil is snug with no pieces sticking up.
3) Make sure the foil isn't within 1" (2.5 cm) of the walls of the oven.

POWER LEVELS:

Most microwave ovens today have variable power. Depending on the model you purchase, there may be anywhere from 1-10 power levels. Similar to the element dials on your conventional oven, you may have set-tings from 1-10 (10 being the highest heat, down to 1 being the lowest heat). (eg): if you had something boiling over on high, you would reduce the heat to 5 or a medium setting. Relate the variable power settings on your microwave oven to the element dials on your conventional oven. Basically, the power levels in a microwave oven are as follows :

<u>FULL POWER</u> : is the highest setting; also referred to as "high", "power level 10", or "100% power".

<u>MEDIUM-HIGH POWER</u> : a "medium-high" setting, "between power levels 6-8" or "60-80% power".

<u>MEDIUM POWER</u> : "½ power", "power level 5" or "50% power". This however may be set at 70-80% in some older ovens so: * check your "use & care manual." In my recipes "medium is 50%", so if your oven is set "higher" on medium, just turn it down "medium-low".

<u>MEDIUM-LOW POWER</u> : this can be your "defrost" cycle, "power level 3-4" or "30-40% power".

<u>LOW POWER</u>: this is the lowest setting on your dial; also referred to as "warm", or in some ovens : "defrost", "power level 1", or "10% power".

<u>TO DETERMINE COOKING TIMES</u>:
This is perhaps the area that is most frustrating for a lot of people. The

INTRODUCTION

more that goes into a microwave oven, the
longer the cooking time. The less that goes
in, the shorter the time. Most foods cook by
weight .... so if you know the "magic cooking times".... you're all set! I find a
KITCHEN SCALE invaluable with the use
of the microwave oven. What affects the
cooking time is the weight of all the moisture going into the oven. That would be the
chicken in the sauce or the potatoes with
their water. The WEIGHT of the dish does
not affect the cooking time, so don't include it. Some dishes (ie: Corning, Pyrex,
pottery etc.) will take on heat from the
food & get hot. In this case the food may
take a little longer to cook, but this is taken
into consideration with the variance in cooking time in casseroles (ie: 7-9 minutes) & with
the standing time.

Allow:

Poultry: 6 min./lb. (13 min./kg.) on high heat
for stir frying.

or : 9 min./lb. (18 min./kg.) on medium
for roasting.

Vegetables: 6 min./lb. (13 min./kg.) on high
(covered) with ¼" water for root
vegetables.

Fruit : 6 min./lb. (13 min./kg.) on high (covered).

INTRODUCTION

<u>Ground meats</u>: (ground beef, chicken, turkey or pork): 6 min./lb. (13 min./kg.) on high

<u>Red meats</u>: 9-14 min./lb. (18-28 min./kg.) on medium ... variance in time allows for rare to well done meat.

<u>Seafood</u>: 4 min./lb. (8 min./kg.) on high.

* A casserole with cooked ingredients to serve a family of 4-6, will take 6-10 minutes cooking on high heat & covered with wax paper.

* If you cut a recipe in half, it will only need half the cooking time. If you double a recipe, it will take almost double the time.

* See (Back Cover) for a list of some "Basic Timings".

<u>STANDING TIME</u>:
     "Standing time", often known as "carry over cooking time, is probably the most important thing you should know about microwaving. I would prefer to call it "the buffer zone"! Because all microwaves cook at different speeds, & because the voltage coming into your

home will vary throughout the day, & be-cause microwaves cook so fast, it is safer to allow the food to "stand" (either inside the oven or out) after the cooking time. I allow 5-10 minutes for all seafood, vegetables & casseroles & 5-10 minutes for all meats. This is especially important for all foods high in bacteria. The air inside the micro-wave oven is not hot & the fan circulating the air can tend to keep the outside sur-face of the food at a lower temperature. Steam will burn your skin, so it stands to reason that if the food sits under a lid, it will continue to cook. Think of the egg in the skillet on top of the stove.... when the egg is done, you can turn the element off, you can even take the skillet off the el-ement... BUT... if you leave the egg in that hot pan for any length of time, it will con-tinue to cook. This is "standing time."

REHEATING:

There is no hard & fast rule I can give for reheating, as it really depends on the ingredients & how cold the food is. If the food has not come from the fridge, reheat on high power. If the food has come from the fridge reheat on medium-high power, (power level 8 or 80% power). The best tip I can give you is: remember... the centre of

the food is the last to heat up & the food will eventually make the dish hot. So ....
feel the bottom of the dish in the middle & you'll be able to tell if the food is hot enough to serve : "GUIDE"

one plate (reheat)	1-2 min. covered
one plate (cold → reheat)	2½-3½ min. covered
casserole (for 4-6 reheat)	4-6 min. covered
casserole (for 4-6 cold → reheat)	8-10 min. covered

DEFROSTING:

In most cases this is 30% power but in others it may be 50% power. However, you can defrost at a lower setting if you find your oven's defrost cycle is too fast for certain foods.

DEFROST CYCLE: basically, as the microwave oven defrosts, it warms up the outside edges of the food which then start to melt the ice crystals in the food. Near the end of the cycle you may find the outside edges will start cooking ... you can slow up this process by turning the oven off & breaking away the cooked edges. Remember, everything that defrosts in the microwave oven should have a "HOLDING TIME" - after defrosting & before cooking. This allows the temperature to become uniform throughout. Holding time = Defrost time so if it takes 15 minutes to defrost a roast, you really shouldn't cook it for another 15 min.

SUGGESTED MENUS

a.	Couscous P. 86 Ratatouille P. 85 Thai Turkey Balls P. 57 Lemon Cake P. 103	b.	Salmon Loaves P.66 Scalloped Potatoes P. 79 Peas P. 74-75 Poppy Seed Cake P. 104
c.	Hawaiian Chicken P. 54 Rice P. 87-90 Carrots au Gratin P.83 Orange Cake P. 103	d.	Chili P.47 Cornbread P. 114 Tossed Salad Baked Apples P.92
e.	Burgers P. 60-61 Potato Wedges P. 80 Stuffed Peppers P. 84 Chocolate Pudding P.107	f.	Carrot Soup P. 32 Tuna Light Lunch P.63 Baked or Fresh Fruit P. 94
g.	Minestrone Soup P. 34 Hobo Bread P. 111 Snack 'N Cake P. 100	h.	Seafood Ratatouille P.67 Rice P. 87-90 OR Pasta P. 70 Hovis Bread P. 112 Feather Cake P.99
i.	Beef Stew P.59 Hovis Bread P. 112 Stewed Rhubarb P.104	j.	Meatballs P. 60-61 Teriyaki Sauce P.62 Swedish Potatoes P.78 Vegetable Toss P. 77
k.	Chicken Casserole P.53 Corn Bread P. 114 Tossed Salad Baked Fruit P. 94	l.	Steak P.41 Roast Potatoes P. 81 Corn on the Cob P. 76 Fruit Crisp P.95
m.	Lamb Chops P.40 Parslied Potatoes P. 82 Scalloped Cabbage P. 84 Baked Apples P. 92	n.	Curried Chicken P.56 Rice P. 87-90 Vegetable Toss P. 77 White Cake P.102
o.	Coq au Vin P. 52 Pasta P. 70 Green Beans P. 74-75 Feather Cake P.99	p.	Pork Chops P.40 Baked Apple Slices P.93 Roast Potatoes P. 81 Broccoli P. 74-75

TIPS ON SODIUM & FAT

The recipes in this book were made with only low fat products (skim or 1% milk, soft margarine, low fat cheese etc.) To further reduce sodium in any of the recipes, use "fresh" ingredients rather than canned. You should also be aware of the following sodium contents :

Low fat Mozarella Cheese has:132mg /28g of Sodium
Low fat Cheddar Cheese has:1540mg/100g of Sodium
Regular Cheddar Cheese has: 620 mg/100g of Sodium

Bread crumbs, cracker crumbs, light soy sauce & Parmesan cheese are also high in Sodium.

Light Sour Cream has : 53mg /100g of sodium
Light Cottage Cheese has: 418 mg/100g of sodium

BUT: The fat content of latter two are as follows:

Light Sour Cream has : 7g /100g of fat
Light Cottage Cheese has : 1g /100g of fat

* Look for "TIPS" & "HEART SMART TIPS" throughout the book.

READY? SET? LET'S MICROWAVE IT!

SODIUM · FREE RECIPES:

The following are reprinted with permission from the 1984 British Columbia Diet/Nutritional Care manual:

INGREDIENTS	AMOUNT	DIRECTIONS

SODIUM-FREE BAKING POWDER:

INGREDIENTS	AMOUNT	DIRECTIONS
Tartaric Acid	7.5g	Have a pharmacist make up
Potassium Bitartrate	56.1g	the recipe. Use 7ml (1½tsp.)
Potassium Bicarbonate	39.8g	of mixture in place of regu-
Cornstarch	28.0g	lar baking powder. Add this
		baking powder toward the
Note: This preparation		end of mixing time & stir
is high in potassium.		only enough to mix.

SODIUM- FREE MUSTARD:

INGREDIENTS	AMOUNT	DIRECTIONS
Vinegar	250 ml (1cup)	make a paste of dry ingred-
Dry mustard	125 ml (½ cup)	ients & 125 ml (½ cup) vine-
White sugar	15 ml (1 tbsp.)	gar. Heat remaining vinegar.
Cornstarch	20 ml (4 tsp.)	(*) Add paste to heated
Pepper	2 ml (½tsp.)	vinegar & cook in double
Yellow Food Colouring (optional)		boiler (*) until thick. Store
		in refrigerator.

SODIUM-FREE TOMATO KETCHUP:

INGREDIENTS	AMOUNT	DIRECTIONS
Unsalted canned toma-to or peeled, quartered fresh tomato	1000 ml (4 cups)	Simmer tomato & onion un-til soft. (*) Process 1-2 min.
Onion, chopped	200ml (¾ cup)	in blender. Add remaining
White sugar	50ml (¼ cup)	ingredients & simmer approx-
Vinegar	125ml (½ cup)	imately 1½ hours (*) until
Ground cloves	1ml (¼tsp.)	reduced to ½ original volume.
Ginger	1ml (¼tsp.)	Add cornstarch to 50ml (¼cup)
Chili powder	0.5ml (⅛tsp.)	of mixture, & return to pot
Cinnamon	1ml (¼ tsp.)	until sauce thickened (*)
Allspice	1ml (¼tsp.)	(stir constantly) Store in
Cornstarch	15ml (1tbsp.)	refrigerator.

(*) These steps can be done in the microwave oven.

SOUPS & SNACKS

CARROT PATÉ

This wonderful appetizer or sandwich spread has been adapted from one of Mignon Lundmark's vegetarian menus. It is easy to prepare & "so good for you"!

onion	½ cup	125 ml
carrot, sliced	2	2
orange juice	¼ cup	50 ml
orange peel, optional	2 tsp.	10 ml
pepper	¼ tsp.	1 ml
cayenne pepper	⅛ tsp.	0.5 ml
or curry powder	⅛ tsp.	0.5 ml
light Miracle Whip	2 tbsp.	30 ml
prepared mustard	½ tsp.	2 ml

1: Combine the first six ingredients in a covered casserole. Cook on high heat 5-7 min. (6 min./lb. or 13 min./kg.) Stir & let stand 10 min. If vegetables are not soft after standing time, cook a little longer.

2: Drain, reserving the stock. Pureé the vegetable mixture adding back a little stock if needed.

3: When the mixture is cool, stir in the Miracle Whip & mustard, then chill. Serve as a spread or as a dip with crackers or triangles of toasted whole wheat bread.

per tbsp:

Dietary Fibre 0.2 Cholesterol 0 mg Carbohydrate 2 g
Total Fat 0 g Unsaturated Fat 0.4 Sodium 14 mg
Energy 10 kCal Protein 0 g Calcium 3 mg Iron 0.1 mg

CHEESE BITES

So fast ... so easy ... so good!

light cheddar cheese, grated	½ cup	125 ml
light Miracle Whip	¼ cup	50 ml
Worcestershire sauce	⅛ tsp.	0.5 ml
prepared mustard	½ tsp.	2 ml
chopped green onion	1	1

1: Blend cheese, Miracle Whip, Worcestershire sauce & mustard.
2: Spread mixture on crackers or triangles of toasted whole wheat bread. Top with green onion pieces ... don't overstack or it will just run off when melted.
3: Cook uncovered, 30-45 sec. on high heat. Serve immediately. (See Tip P. 21).

per tbsp:

Dietary Fibre 0.0 Cholesterol 12 mg Carbohydrate 2 g
Total Fat 2 g Unsaturated Fat 1.9 Sodium 165 mg
Energy 37 kCal Protein 2 g Calcium 41 mg Iron 0.1 mg

ONION CANAPÉS

green onion, chopped	⅓ cup	75 mL
light Miracle Whip	¼ cup	50 mL
grated Parmesan cheese	2 tbsp.	30 mL

1: Mix all ingredients & spread on crackers or triangles of toasted whole wheat bread.
2: Cook uncovered, 45 sec. - 1 min. on high heat. Serve immediately.

per tbsp:

Dietary Fibre 0.1 Cholesterol 4 mg Carbohydrate 2 g
Total Fat 3 g Unsaturated Fat 2.6 Sodium 105 mg
Energy 42 kCal Protein 1 g Calcium 28 mg Iron 0.1 mg

ARTICHOKE DIP

	14 oz. can	398 ml can
artichokes		
light Miracle Whip	½ cup	125 ml
Parmesan cheese	½ cup	125 ml
garlic powder	½ tsp.	2 ml

1: Drain & chop the artichokes.
2: Combine all ingredients in an onion soup bowl or similar-sized pot.
3: Cook 3-5 minutes on high until heated through. Serve with crackers or triangles of toasted whole wheat bread.

per tbsp:

Dietary Fibre 0.3 Cholesterol 2 mg Carbohydrate 2 g
Total Fat 1 g Unsaturated Fat 0.8 Sodium 52 mg
Energy 20 kCal Protein 1 g Calcium 20 mg Iron 0.2 mg

Variation: use the same quantity of cooked onions, leeks, broccoli, spinach etc. instead of artichokes.

VEGETABLE DIP

low fat cottage cheese	I cup	250 ml
lemon juice	I tbsp.	15 ml
skim milk	2 tbsp.	30 ml
dill weed	2 tsp.	10 ml
minced onion	2 tsp.	10 ml

1: Blenderize all ingredients until creamy.
2: Serve with fresh vegetables or try "parcooking" them for a nice variation.

per tbsp:

Dietary Fibre 0.0 Cholesterol 1 mg Carbohydrate 1 g
Total Fat 0 g Unsaturated Fat 0.0 Sodium 53 mg
Energy 10 kCal Protein 2 g Calcium 12 mg Iron 0.1 mg

TORTILLA ROLL

This is a quick & easy appetizer or snack. Save remaining soft tortilla shells for main courses with meat or vegetable fillings (See P. 44-47, 85).

soft tortilla shells	1-2	1-2
light cream cheese or yogurt cheese (See P.122)	2 tbsp.	30ml
salmon, mashed	1 can (7¾oz.)	1 can (220g)
green onion, chopped	1	1
salsa sauce	2 Tbsp	30 mL

1: Spread tortilla shell with yogurt cheese & then spread with mashed salmon, sprinkle with green onion & spread with salsa sauce.
2: Roll the tortilla shells up & wrap with wax paper & chill for several hours.
3: Cut across the roll making thin slices. Serve on a bed of lettuce.

per tortilla:

Dietary Fibre 0.2   Cholesterol 19 mg   Carbohydrate 8 g
Total Fat 8 g Unsaturated Fat 5.5 Sodium 228 mg
Energy 156 kCal   Protein 12 g   Calcium 132 mg   Iron 1.0 mg

Use puréed low fat cottage cheese or yogurt cheese (P. 122) in place of sour cream or cream cheese in your recipes.

BEAN DIP

beans in tomato sauce	1 (14oz.) can	1 (398ml) can
cheddar cheese, grated	½ cup	125 ml
garlic powder	1 tsp.	5 ml
chili powder	1 tsp.	5 ml
cayenne pepper	⅛ tsp.	0.5 ml
vinegar	2 tsp.	10 ml
Worcestershire sauce	2 tsp.	10 ml

1: Pureé beans in a blender or food processor.
2: Combine all ingredients & cook on high
   heat 2½-3½ min. or until heated through,
   & cheese melts.
3: Serve with low fat tortilla crisps, toasted
   pita wedges or low fat crackers.

per tbsp:

Dietary Fibre 0.3   Cholesterol 3 mg   Carbohydrate 3 g
Total Fat 0 g Unsaturated Fat 0.1 Sodium 81 mg
Energy 16 kCal Protein 1 g Calcium 17 mg Iron 0.1 mg

Variation: layer on toasted pita wedges or
      tortilla rounds & top with chopped tomato
      & a sprinkle of cheese. Use leftover dip in
      "Burritos" (P. 44-45).

Low fat cheddar cheese has 2½ times
more sodium than regular cheddar
cheese! (See Tip. P. 21)

Watch out for hidden fat in foods...
many crackers, cookies, granola &
snacks are high in fat ... Read those labels!

SOUPS & STEWS:

FREEZER : leftovers become "planned overs"! If you have lots of freezer space, line your favorite casserole with plastic wrap or freezer bag & fill the dish with a serving(s) of the food. Once frozen, you can lift it out of the dish, wrap it well & store it in the freezer for a later date. This way you don't tie up your dishes in the freezer & when you are ready for the food, it will fit right back into the dish for defrosting & heating. This trick can also be used for leftover casseroles, rice & pasta.

REHEATING FROZEN FOODS: frozen foods must be defrosted before heating. Most foods should be defrosted on the "defrost" cycle. I allow 6 min./lb. (4 min./kg.). This does not totally defrost the food, but gets it started. If you put your food in the microwave oven until it is totally defrosted, you'll end up "cooking" the outside edges ... instead, allow your food to stand for a time equal to the defrost time...(eg) if it takes 18 minutes to defrost your food, don't cook it for another 18 minutes, to allow the temperature to become uniform throughout.

REHEATING : to reheat a bowl of soup, heat 1½ - 2½ minutes on high. As the outside edges will heat first, it's a good idea to stir once from the outside to the centre.

PROBE: if you want to use your temperature probe to reheat your soup, set it
for 160° for a water-base soup & 150° for a
cream-base soup... (follow your manufacturer's instructions for setting the probe). Your
oven will shut off or go to a "hold" setting
when the food reaches the right temperature,
& it will be ready to eat!

* The probe can also be used for heating hot drinks, casseroles or cooking meats.

SOUP STOCK, SOUPS OR STEWS:

Make your favorite recipe ... you don't
need special microwave recipes! Remember,
a boil is a boil & to simmer, just turn the
heat down .... the microwave is just another cooking appliance. The advantage of the
microwave oven (other than obvious energy
savings) is that because there is no direct
heat on the bottom of the cooking dish, there's
no burning or scorching. The foods get even
heat from all sides.

Soups or stews that take 2-3 hours on
top of a stove will take ⅓ of the time in
the microwave .... that means 45 minutes -
1 hour in the microwave! You can freeze
leftover stock in ice cube trays to use later
or instead of water in recipes (rice, sauces etc)

Make your own soup stock: that way
you have more control of what is in it!

If you don't have homemade soup stock, you can use low sodium bouillon cubes or powder. These are added to water to make stock.

You can make a wonderful vegetable stock by cooking up an onion, carrot & celery. You can adjust the flavor by increasing or decreasing the proportion of onion to the other vegetables. I put one of each (or more if needed) in a covered casserole with 1 cup (250 mL) of water. Cook on high heat for 8-10 minutes. Let stand & purée.

DRY SOUP MIXES:

These need time to rehydrate & therefore take almost as long as the conventional method.

1: Prepare soup according to package directions.
2: Cook covered on high 3-4 minutes.
3: Let stand covered for 5 minutes of "carry over cooking time".

CANNED SOUP:

Heat 1½- 2 minutes / bowl on high heat.

Remember.... "processed" foods are often high in fat & /or salt.

CARROT SOUP

This is a wonderful soup! ... & it's good hot or cold. Dill weed is one of my favorite spices ... but ... for a nice change see the variations below.

carrots, chopped	2 cups	250 mL
onion, chopped	⅓ cup	175 ml
chicken stock (low sodium)	2 cups	250 ml
pepper	- to taste -	
dry dill weed	1 tsp.	5 ml
milk (low fat)	¼ cup	50 ml

1: Combine the carrots, onion, pepper & ½ the chicken stock in a covered casserole. Cook on high heat for 15 minutes. If the mixture starts to boil over in the casserole you're using, then turn down the heat.

2: Purée the mixture & add the remaining ingredients. Cook on high heat another 2-3 minutes.

per ¾ cup serving:

Dietary Fibre 1.6   Cholesterol 2 mg   Carbohydrate 9 g
Total Fat 5 g   Unsaturated Fat 1.1   Sodium 28 mg
Energy 96 kCal   Protein 5 g   Calcium 54 mg   Iron 0.8 mg

Variations: (instead of using dill weed)

Ginger Carrot Soup : ⅛-½ tsp. (0.5-2ml) ginger

Curried Carrot Soup: ½-1 tsp. (2-5ml) curry

"TIP

Most fish markets have a "FISH STOCK mix" gathered from fish trimmings. This is a wonderful base for any fish soup... eg: seafood chowder.

HAWAIIAN CHICKEN P. 54

CREAM OF CELERY SOUP

Why is it that we always buy more celery than its refrigerator life allows? When that celery starts to look as if it won't last much longer, put it in a margarine container in the freezer. When you're ready to make soup or a celery sauce, defrost this limp product & once puréed it adds incredible flavor to many dishes.... it's a good base for celery soup too!

celery, chopped	- 3 stalks -	
potato, peeled & chopped	- 1 medium -	
onion, chopped	1/3 cup	75 ml
chicken stock, (low sodium)	2 cups	500 ml
pepper	- to taste -	
dried parsley	1 tsp.	5 ml
milk (low fat)	1/2 cup	125 ml

1: Combine the celery, potato, onion, pepper, parsley & 1 cup (250 ml) of the chicken stock in a covered casserole. Cook on high heat for 15 minutes. If the mixture wants to boil over, turn the heat down.

2: Purée the mixture & add the last cup of stock & the milk. Heat on high another 2-3 minutes.

per 3/4 cup serving:

Dietary Fibre 1.0   Cholesterol 2 mg   Carbohydrate 8 g
Total Fat 5 g Unsaturated Fat 1.0 Sodium 42 mg
Energy 92 kCal Protein 5 g Calcium 64 mg Iron 0.6 mg

MINESTRONE SOUP

Quick, easy & very healthy! You can use fresh tomatoes in this to reduce sodium content.

Beef bouillon cubes (low sodium)	- 2 -	
water	2 cups	500 ml
pasta, shells, alphabets	¼ cup	50 ml
potato, cubed	- 1 -	
celery, sliced	- 1 stalk -	
carrot, peeled & sliced	½ cup	125 ml
zucchini, sliced	½ cup	125 ml
green beans	½ cup	125 ml
tomatoes	14 oz. can	398 ml can
basil	½ tsp.	2 ml

1: Combine all ingredients in a large casserole & cook on high for 20-25 minutes.
2: Stir half way through the cooking time.

per ¾ cup serving:

*Dietary Fibre 1.7 Cholesterol 1 mg Carbohydrate 11 g
Total Fat 3 g Unsaturated Fat 0.8 Sodium 137 mg
Energy 89 kCal Protein 4 g Calcium 42 mg Iron 1.1 mg*

Variation: you may want to skip all the vegetables & throw in "leftovers" or some frozen mixed vegetables.

TIP
If celery, parsley etc. start to go limp in the fridge, they can be frozen, then later on puréed & added to soups, stews & sauces.

TIP
There is no "scorching" in the microwave ∴ no need to stir as often.

CHICKEN VEGETABLE SOUP

I use fresh, uncooked chicken breast meat that I have skinned & boned.

onion, chopped	⅓ cup	75 ml
chicken stock	3 cups	750 ml
carrot, chopped	½ cup	125 ml
potato, chopped	– 1 small –	
celery, chopped	½ cup	125 ml
chicken, chopped	¼ lb.	125 g
pasta or rice	¼ cup	50 ml
parsley	1 tbsp.	15 ml

1: Combine all ingredients in a large casserole. Cook on high heat for 20-25 minutes, stirring once. (Remember... if anything wants to boil over in the microwave oven, just turn the heat down as you would for elements on top of the stove).

per ¾ cup serving:

Dietary Fibre 0.9   Cholesterol 12 mg   Carbohydrate 8 g
Total Fat 4 g Unsaturated Fat 0.1 Sodium 27 mg
Energy 101 kCal Protein 10 g Calcium 31 mg Iron 0.8 mg

Variation: "Clean out the fridge soup".... use the above method & all your leftovers to make "Friday Night Soup"!

"Pot" barley is higher in fibre than "Pearl" barley. Try it in the "STOUP" recipe on the following page....
(P. 36).

TIP

STOUP

A hearty, healthy stew or soup. "STOUP" is easy to prepare & very versatile ... clean out the fridge with this one!

pot barley	¼ cup	50 ml
beef or chicken stock (low sodium)	3 cups	750 ml
ground meat	½ lb.	250 g.
onion, chopped	½ cup	125 ml
carrot, chopped	1	1
celery, chopped	½ cup	125 ml
pepper	– to taste –	

1: Combine barley with soup stock. Cook covered, for 10 minutes on high... (turn the power level down if it starts to boil).
2: In a separate casserole, cook ground meat 3-4 minutes on high, stirring 2-3 times to break up the meat as it is cooking. Drain.
3: Combine barley-broth mixture, cooked meat & remaining ingredients. Cook covered, for another 10 minutes on high.

per ¾ cup serving:

Dietary Fibre 1.9   Cholesterol 15 mg   Carbohydrate 10 g
Total Fat 5 g Unsaturated Fat 1.0 Sodium 42 mg
Energy 166 kCal Protein 12 g Calcium 35 mg Iron 1.4 mg

Variations:
- Substitute rice, pasta or potato for barley or use brown rice & barley together.
- use up "leftover" meats & vegetables
- use ground beef, chicken, turkey or veal
- if vegetarian use T.V.P. (see P.41) & vegetable stock in place of meat & beef stock.

MAIN DISHES

STUFFED WHOLE ROASTED CHICKEN

<u>ROASTING WHOLE CHICKEN OR TURKEY</u>:

- Wash poultry & salt cavity if desired.
- Add stuffing, if desired, & secure a crust of bread in the cavity to keep the stuffing from falling out. DON'T use metal skewers, but tie the bird up with butcher's twine.
- Season or glaze the outside of the bird. Diluted kitchen Bouquet or butter & paprika work well for extra browning. Save salting the outside as it tends to dry it out.
- You may want to start a large turkey upside-down. Place the bird on a meat rack & cover with a loose tent of wax paper.
- Allow 9 min./lb. (19½ min./kg.) on half power (level 5, 50% power or medium). Remember... you must add the weight of the stuffing to the weight of the bird ... eg: if you have 1 lb. of stuffing, your 10 lb. bird becomes an 11 lb. bird!
- Half way through the cooking time, check to see if any areas are overcooking. These can be shielded with aluminum foil. (See P. 14).
- After cooking, allow 10-15 minutes of "carry over cooking time". Cover with a casserole or foil to keep it hot while standing.

ROAST OF BEEF OR LAMB

For roasted potatoes with your roast, see (P. 81).

- Place roast, fat side down, on a micro-wave meat rack. Season as desired. Avoid salt as it tends to dry out the meat. Cover with a loose tent of wax paper.
- Always do roasts on ½ power (level 5 or medium). This allows the connective tissue to break down & tenderizes the meat.
- Allow 9-14 mins./lb. (19½ mins./kg.) on ½ power & allow 15 minutes of "carry over cooking time."
- To reheat beef, allow 30-45 seconds per slice, covered with wax paper.
- Serve lamb with mint sauce or jelly.

TEMPERATURE PROBE COOKING:
- Set your probe according to the manu-facturer's directions.
- The tip of the probe should be in the center of the meat, away from bone, fat or air pockets. The usual settings are:
130° - Rare
150° - Medium (also soups & casseroles)
170°-180° - Well done (beef, pork or lamb)

An average meat serving should be no larger than a deck of cards

ROAST PORK

Follow instructions as for roast beef on previous page, but cook to the well done stage.

- Allow 13 min./lb. (28 min./kg.) on ½ power (50%, level 5 or medium). Allow 15 minutes of "carry over cooking time."
- Pork roasts are also nice stuffed.... untie the rolled roast, stuff with your favorite bread stuffing & retie. To determine the cooking time, you must add the weight of the stuffing to the weight of the meat.
- Half way through the cooking time, turn the roast over & apply a glaze of apricot jam or marmalade etc.

PORK OR LAMB CHOPS

Arrange chops on a meat tray or pie plate. Baste with Kitchen Bouquet, paprika, low sodium soy sauce or barbecue sauce (P.63).

I like to lay slices of apple over pork chops & a hint of mint on lamb chops.

Cook on ½ power (50%, level 5 or medium) for 13 min./lb. (28 min./kg.), covered with wax paper.

- 1 chop will take about 3-5 min.
- 2 chops will take about 6-9 min.
- 3 chops will take about 10-13 min.
- 4 chops will take about 13-16 min.

* See Photo P.80a

STEAK

If you like, marinate steak in:

red wine	½ cup	125 ml
olive oil	2 tbsp.	25 ml
soy sauce, low sodium	¼ cup	50 ml
brown sugar	1 tbsp.	15 ml
garlic, optional	½ tsp.	2 ml

1: Place steak on a meat tray or pie plate. Cook on ½ power (50%, level 5 or medium).
   * ½ lb. (250g.) of steak will take about 4-6 minutes, uncovered.

per 3 oz. serving :

Dietary Fibre 0.0   Cholesterol 61 mg   Carbohydrate 0 g
Total Fat 16 g   Unsaturated Fat 10.5   Sodium 111 mg
Energy 342 kCal   Protein 19 g   Calcium 12 mg   Iron 2.9 mg

VEGETARIAN MEAT SUBSTITUTE

T.V.P. (Textured Vegetable Protein) was introduced to me by Mignon Lundmark. It is one of many meat substitutes & it is ideal for those cooking for one. It is purchased at health food stores in dry form & kept on the shelf much like cereal. T.V.P. is made from soy flour, is cholesterol-free & is low in sodium. It can be used in any recipe that calls for ground beef.

To rehydrate:
   1: Boil ⅞ cup (225ml.) water or stock.
   2: Stir in 1 cup (250ml) dry T.V.P.
   3: Let stand 10 min. (It will double in volume).

TACOS

This is a favorite meal in our house! It doesn't matter how busy your day, these can be "whipped up" in no time & on the table to produce a great meal.

ground turkey, chicken or lean ground beef	1/3 lb.	.165 kg.
onion powder	1/2 tsp.	2 ml
chili powder	1/2 tsp.	2 ml
cayenne pepper	− pinch −	
garlic powder	− pinch −	
oregano	− pinch −	
cumin	− pinch −	
water	2 tbsp.	25 ml
tomato, chopped	1	1
lettuce, shredded	1 1/2 cups	375 ml
low fat cheese, optional	1/2 cup	125 ml
tortilla shells, soft or hard	− 2-4 −	

1: Cook ground meat on high for 2 minutes, stopping to stir every 30 seconds to break up the meat. It doesn't matter if you cover the dish or not. This is similar to what you would do if you had the meat in a skillet on top of the stove.

2: Drain the meat & add the 6 seasonings & water. Cover the dish & cook on high heat for another 1 1/2 - 2 minutes.

3: Divide the meat mixture on 2-4 tortilla shells. Top with tomatoes, lettuce & cheese.

per shell, filled :

Dietary Fibre 0.7   Cholesterol 27 mg   Carbohydrate 16 g
Total Fat 2 g Unsaturated Fat 1.0 Sodium 70 mg
Energy 125 kCal Protein 11 g Calcium 74 mg Iron 1.8 mg

* Leftover soft shells make great "crépes" for any fillings you may have (hot or cold), as well as dessert crepes!

* Although Tacos make a meal in themselves, I usually serve them with beans (See P.48-50) & Spanish rice.

MEATLESS TACOS

Substitute the ground meat in the previous TACO recipe with T.V.P. (See P.41)

TACO SALAD

Using corn tortilla chips instead of tortilla shells , "toss" all of the ingredients in the "TACOS" recipe on previous page or... layer the lettuce , then the hot meat mixture, cheese & tomato. Arrange the chips around the edge of a serving dish & serve immediately !
   * This is great for a "Pot Luck" dinner.

MEATLESS TACO SALAD

Just omit the meat in the above recipe !

BURRITOS

lean ground beef	½ lb.	250 g.
onion powder	I tsp.	5 ml
chili powder	½ tsp.	2 ml
garlic powder	½ tsp.	2 ml
soy sauce, low sodium	I tsp.	5 ml
tomato sauce	½ cup	125 ml
refried beans or		
beans in tomato sauce	½ cup	125 ml
tortilla shells, soft·medium size 4		4

1: Cook ground beef on high heat 3-4 minutes, stirring 2-3 times to break up the meat. Drain.
2: Combine the meat, spices, soy sauce, tomato sauce & refried beans. Cook on medium high (power level 8, 80% power) for 4-6 minutes.
3: Heat the shells in a covered casserole for 15-40 seconds.
4: Spoon the filling into the shells, fold up & roll. Arrange in a shallow casserole.
5: Top with ½ cup (125ml) tomato sauce & a sprinkle of low fat cheddar cheese. Cover & heat 45 sec.- 1½ min.

per tortilla, filled:

Dietary Fibre 1.9   Cholesterol 29 mg   Carbohydrate 22 g
Total Fat 9 g   Unsaturated Fat 4.3   Sodium 240 mg
Energy 218 kCal   Protein 14 g   Calcium 80 mg   Iron 2.7 mg

* Other suggested toppings: chopped tomato, shredded lettuce or salsa sauce.
* The above filling can also be used in Taco shells & topped with suggested toppings.

MEATLESS BURRITOS

Use rehydrated T.V.P. (see P. 41) as a substitute for the ground beef. Cook as in Step 2 on previous page.

FAJITAS

A wonderful, easy meal!

flour tortilla shell or whole wheat pita pockets	4	4
filling (see P. 46)	1 lb.	500 g.
onion	½	½
green pepper &/or red pepper	½ ½	½ ½
soy sauce, low sodium	¼ cup	50 ml

1: Thinly slice meat & vegetables.
2: Combine all ingredients, except the shells, in a shallow dish. (If time allows, marinate several hours or overnight).
3: Cook, covered with wax paper, on high heat for 6-8 min., stirring once (6 min/lb. or 13 min./kg.). Let stand for 5 minutes.
4: Roll in tortilla shells, folding up one end or stuff into pita pockets. Serve with salsa sauce.

per tortilla, filled:

Dietary Fibre 1.0   Cholesterol 7 mg   Carbohydrate 18 g
Total Fat 1 g   Unsaturated Fat 0.4   Sodium 442 mg
Energy 95 kCal   Protein 5 g   Calcium 66 mg   Iron 1.3 mg

* See next page for "FILLINGS".... & "MEATLESS FAJITAS".

Fillings for Fajitas (previous page) P. 45
  Chicken : use chicken breast , boned & skinned
  Beef: use extra lean ground beef
  Turkey: use ground turkey or chicken
  Vegetables : use strips of vegetables
  eg: broccoli, carrot, cabbage , mushrooms etc.

MEATLESS FAJITAS

Use rehydrated T.V.P. (See P. 41) as a substitute for meat. Add 2 cups (500ml) of rehydrated T.V.P. as the filling in the FAJITAS recipe on the previous page.

Variation: try a hint of ginger &/or brown
  sugar in the mixture

Hint: extra tortilla shells are great for
  appetizers (See P. 27) or leftovers.

TIP For firmer Tofu; freeze it overnight then defrost, squeeze out excess water & crumble. It will then have a chewier texture, more like ground beef. (Try in "meatless Chili" on opposite page).

TIP Whatever you would cook on top of the stove can be done in the microwave oven ....(except melting paraffin wax....it has no moisture in it.)

EASY CHILI

lean ground beef	½ lb.	250 g.
onion , chopped	½ cup	125 ml
stewed tomatoes or	¾ cup	175 ml
tomatoes , finely chopped	2	2
tomato sauce	¾ cup	175 ml
beans in tomato sauce or kidney beans	¾ cup	175 ml
chili powder	2 tsp.	10 ml
green pepper , optional	¼ cup	50 ml
mushrooms , optional	¼ cup	50 ml

1: Combine crumbled beef & onion in a covered casserole. Cook on high heat 2-3 min. stirring once or twice to break up the meat. Drain.

2: Combine the remaining ingredients. Cook covered, 3-5 minutes on high heat. Let stand 5 minutes.

per cup:

> *Dietary Fibre 4.6   Cholesterol 41 mg   Carbohydrate 24 g*
> *Total Fat 12 g   Unsaturated Fat 5.6   Sodium 579 mg*
> *Energy 266 kCal   Protein 18 g   Calcium 56 mg   Iron 2.7 mg*

MEATLESS CHILI

Use rehydrated T.V.P. (See P.41) as a substitute for meat in the above recipe. Use ½ cup (125ml) dry & rehydrate with just less than ½ cup (125ml) of boiling water, tomato juice or stock... OR... add 1 cup (250ml) of drained & chopped "tofu" as a meat substitute. See "TIP" on previous page.

BEANS... a healthy new image.

There is a variety of beans in the market place. Although they vary in taste, they are interchangeable in recipes. They are an excellent source of DIETARY FIBRE: studies have shown that foods high in fibre (beans, peas, lentils, wheat bran, vegetables, fruits, whole grains & breads) can protect us against certain cancers. There are also studies which show that soluble fibre (the kind found in beans, peas, oat bran, fruits & lentils) may help lower your blood cholesterol level. They have NO CHOLESTEROL & are high in PROTEIN. However, the protein in dry beans is low in one of the essential amino acids, so is best served with corn, grains, meat, eggs, cheese or nuts. They are high in VITAMINS, MINERALS & COMPLEX CARBOHYDRATES (which makes them a good source of energy)!

DRY BEANS, PEAS & LENTILS:

SOAK: Beans & whole peas should be soaked before cooking. Rinse & discard any foreign matter. Soak covered in water, in a covered casserole overnight. Drain.

COOK: For 1 cup (250ml) of beans or peas

allow 2½ cups (625 ml) of water. Combine in a 4 quart (4 L.) covered casserole. Cook on high heat 10 minutes & then on medium heat (level 5, 50%) for another 30 minutes or until fork-tender. Stir once or twice during cooking. I usually cook up the beans in the morning & then they have a good long standing time. Later they can be reheated.

HEAT: one cup will only take about 30 seconds – 1 minute to heat, or ... 1½ - 2½ minutes on medium high if they have come from the fridge.

* Of course you can buy beans that are canned & ready to use, but be aware that most are relatively high in sodium.

* It is also important to note that in days gone by, people often added baking soda to beans to help soften them more quickly. Although this is tried & true, it does destroy many of the "B" vitamins.

Try to eat lots of whole grains & vegetables.

SWEET & SOUR BEANS

Beans... a healthy new profile.

brown sugar	2 tbsp.	25 ml
lemon juice	1 tbsp.	15 ml
soy sauce, low sodium	1 tbsp.	15 ml
pineapple chunks	⅓ cup	75 ml
carrot, sliced	⅓ cup	75 ml
celery, sliced	⅓ cup	75 ml
onion, sliced	¼ cup	50 ml
kidney beans	¾ cup	175 ml
chick peas	¾ cup	175 ml

1: Combine all ingredients (except the beans & peas) in a covered casserole. Cook on high heat 2-4 minutes or until vegetables are tender.

2: Stir in beans & peas. Thicken with 1 tbsp. (15 ml) of cornstarch if necessary. Cook on high heat another 2-3 minutes or until heated through. Serve on a bed of rice.

per cup:

Dietary Fibre 2.9 Cholesterol 2 mg Carbohydrate 35 g
Total Fat 1 g Unsaturated Fat 0.9 Sodium 205 mg
Energy 173 kCal Protein 7 g Calcium 61 mg Iron 2.5 mg

* If you have freezer space, double this recipe & freeze the "planned-overs"!

* You can substitute other beans for the kidney beans & chick peas ... I often use navy beans, & if you wanted, you could also use beans in tomato sauce.

CHICKEN STEW

chicken breast	1	1
potatoes, chopped	2	2
carrot, chopped	1	1
onion, chopped	½ cup	125 ml
light chicken stock	1 tbsp.	15 ml
water	1 cup	250 ml
dried parsley, basil or tarragon	1 tsp.	5 ml
pepper		- to taste -

1: Bone & skin the chicken, then cut it into chunks.
2: Scrub & chop the potatoes & carrot.
3: Combine all the ingredients in a covered casserole. Cook on high heat 15-20 minutes. Let stand 5-10 minutes.

* This makes a wonderful meal with fresh bread (See P.110).

per cup:

Dietary Fibre 1.6   Cholesterol 19 mg   Carbohydrate 16 g
Total Fat 1 g   Unsaturated Fat 0.4   Sodium 27 mg
Energy 108 kCal   Protein 10 g   Calcium 18 mg   Iron 1.0 mg

Taste foods before salting... better yet, replace salt with a spice or herb eg: dill weed tarragon, pepper etc.

Trim fat from meat & skin chicken before cooking.

COQ-AU-VIN

"Chicken with wine" for that special occasion.... a delicious & easy recipe shared by Norma Walsh, converted slightly to eliminate fat. If you have the time, assemble this in advance & let the chicken marinate in the casserole several hours or overnight.

chicken pieces	4	4
flour	2 tbsp.	25 ml
red wine	¼ cup	50 ml
chicken stock, low sodium	¼ cup	50 ml
parsley	1 tbsp.	15 ml
garlic powder	¼ tsp.	1 ml
bay leaf	1	1
thyme	⅛ tsp.	.5 ml
pepper	⅛ tsp.	.5 ml
mushrooms, sliced	4	4
onion, sliced	½ cup	125 ml

1: Skin chicken & arrange in a pie plate or 8" casserole dish.
2: Combine the remaining ingredients & pour over the chicken.
3: When ready, cook on high heat, covered with wax paper, 9-13 minutes ... (6 min./lb. or 13 min./kg.). Stir half way through the cooking time. Let stand covered for 5 minutes.

per chicken piece:

Dietary Fibre 1.3   Cholesterol 62 mg   Carbohydrate 13 g
Total Fat 4 g Unsaturated Fat 2.2 Sodium 70 mg
Energy 176 kCal Protein 17 g Calcium 36 mg Iron 2.3 mg

CHICKEN & RICE CASSEROLE

A wonderful meal in one dish... for company, double the recipe & double the time!

long grain rice	½ cup	125 ml
stewed tomatoes	1 (14 oz. can)	1 (398 ml can)
onion, chopped	½ cup	125 ml
green pepper, chopped	½	½
parsley flakes	2 tsp.	10 ml
garlic powder	¼ tsp.	1 ml
pepper	- to taste -	
chicken pieces, skinned	1 lb.	500 g.
Parmesan cheese, optional	¼ cup	50 ml
paprika	1 tsp.	5 ml

1: Combine rice, tomatoes, onion, pepper, parsley, garlic & pepper in an 8" casserole.
2: Arrange chicken pieces over the rice mixture. Sprinkle with cheese & paprika.
3: Cook on ½ power (level 5 or medium), covering with plastic wrap (turn back a corner to allow a steam vent). Cook for 15-25 minutes. Let stand for 10 minutes "carry over cooking time".

per ½ cup rice with 1 chicken piece:

*Dietary Fibre 2.9   Cholesterol 47 mg   Carbohydrate 18 g
Total Fat 3 g   Unsaturated Fat 1.6   Sodium 158 mg
Energy 144 kCal   Protein 14 g   Calcium 31 mg   Iron 2.1 mg*

Variations:

- Try with Cajun, Mexican or Italian stewed tomatoes.
- For Mushroom/Chicken & rice, omit tomatoes & add 1 can of cream of mushroom soup & 1 cup (250ml) of sliced tomatoes.

HAWAIIAN CHICKEN

An easy "make ahead"... serve with rice.

See Photo P. 32a

chicken pieces, skinned	4	4
pineapple chunks	½ cup	125 ml
juice from pineapple	⅓ cup	75 ml
honey	¼ cup	50 ml
ground ginger	⅛ tsp.	.5 ml
soy sauce, low sodium	1 tbsp.	15 ml
cornstarch	1 tbsp.	15 ml
paprika	- sprinkle -	

1: Arrange chicken pieces in an 8" pie plate or casserole. Top with pineapple chunks.

2: Combine the remaining ingredients, except the paprika. Pour mixture over the chicken. (If time permits, marinate the chicken in the sauce for several hours or overnight). Sprinkle paprika over top.

3: Cook on high heat, covered with wax paper, for 6 min./lb. (13 min./kg.)... & add an extra 3-5 minutes to simmer the ingredients. This quantity will take 10-15 minutes & allow a standing time of 5-10 minutes.

per chicken piece:

Dietary Fibre 0.4   Cholesterol 27 mg   Carbohydrate 22 g
Total Fat 1 g   Unsaturated Fat 0.8   Sodium 141 mg
Energy 123 kCal   Protein 7 g   Calcium 12 mg   Iron 0.6 mg

TIP

When cooking a full meal, start with whatever takes the longest to do.... desserts such as baked apples can cook while you're eating dinner.

CRUMB COATED CHICKEN

Chicken pieces	1 or 2	1 or 2
olive oil	2 tbsp.	30 ml
egg whites	2	2
Corn flakes, crushed	¾ cup	175 ml
paprika	- sprinkle -	
pepper, optional	- sprinkle -	

1: Skin chicken & dip in oil or beaten egg whites. Roll in crumbs until evenly coated.

2: Arrange on a meat tray. Sprinkle with plenty of paprika for color & a dash of pepper (optional).

3: Cover with wax paper & cook on high heat 2-4 minutes. (6 min./lb or 13 min/kg.) Let stand 5 minutes.

per chicken piece:

Dietary Fibre 0.5 g Cholesterol 26 mg Carbohydrate 15 g
Total Fat 10 g Unsaturated Fat 9.0 g Sodium 245 mg
Energy 194 kCal Protein 12 g Calcium 6 mg Iron 2.7 mg

Variations:

* Substitute seasoned bread crumbs for corn flake crumbs.

* CRUMB COATED FISH: substitute fish fillets for chicken, however, remember fish cooks much faster ... allow 4 min/lb. or 8.8 min./kg.

CURRIED CHICKEN

apple, chopped	1	1
onion, chopped	1/3 cup	75 ml
curry powder	1 tsp.	5 ml
mushrooms, sliced	1/2 cup	125 ml
milk, low fat	1 cup	250 ml
flour	2 tbsp.	30 ml
pepper	- to taste	-
chicken pieces, skinned	4	4
paprika	- sprinkle	-

1: Combine apple, onion, curry & mushrooms in a pie plate or shallow casserole. Cover with a lid or plastic wrap & cook on high heat 1½-2 minutes.

2: Whisk the milk, flour & pepper together & add to above mixture. Mix well.

3: Arrange chicken pieces in the dish & "smother" them with the sauce.

4: Sprinkle liberally with paprika, cover with wax paper & cook on high heat for 15-20 minutes. Let stand 10 minutes.

per chicken piece:

Dietary Fibre 1.5   Cholesterol 25 mg   Carbohydrate 13 g
Total Fat 6 g Unsaturated Fat 4.1 Sodium 67 mg
Energy 39 kCal Protein 11 g Calcium 104 mg Iron 1.9 mg

CURRIED BEEF

1: Cook ½ lb (250 g.) lean ground beef in a casserole 3-4 min., stirring twice. Drain.

2: Following "CURRIED CHICKEN" recipe above, add the beef in "STEP 3" & cook 5-10 min. (you may enjoy ½ cup (125 ml) of raisins in this too!)

THAI TURKEY BALLS

Make these small to be served as an appetizer OR larger as a part of a main course. I serve these with "COUSCOUS" (See P. 86) & "RATATOUILLE" (See P. 85)

ground turkey	½ lb.	250 g.
soy sauce, low sodium	1½ tsp.	7 ml
chili powder	½ tsp.	2 ml
olive oil	¼ tsp.	1 ml
water	¼ cup.	50 ml
brown sugar	¼ cup	50 ml
lemon juice	¼ cup	50 ml
onion powder	½ tsp.	2 ml
chopped medium chilies, drained	1 (4 oz.) can	1 (125 g) can

1: Mix together turkey, soy sauce, chili powder & oil. Shape into balls & arrange on a microwave meat tray or pie plate.

2: Cook, covered with wax paper, for 2-3 minutes on high heat. Let stand for 5 minutes. Drain.

3: In a mixing bowl, combine the remaining ingredients. Pour over meatballs & heat, uncovered, another 1-1½ minutes.

per meatball:

Dietary Fibre 0.3   Cholesterol 23 mg   Carbohydrate 8 g
Total Fat 2 g   Unsaturated Fat 1.7   Sodium 65 mg
Energy 41 kCal   Protein 8 g   Calcium 14 mg   Iron 0.9 mg

* For softer meatballs, stir in 2 tbsp. (30 ml) of applesauce to "STEP 1" ingredients.

SHEPHERD'S PIE

An easy rendition of an old favorite.

potatoes	2	2
lean ground beef (chicken, lamb etc)	½ lb.	250 g.
onion, chopped	½ cup	125 ml.
garlic powder	¼ tsp.	1 ml.
pepper	- dash	-
parsley	1 tbsp.	15 ml.
mushrooms, chopped	½ cup	125 ml
prepared mustard	1 tsp.	5 ml
flour	1 tbsp.	15 ml
milk	½ cup	125 ml
water or red wine	¼ cup	50 ml

1: Pierce & bake potatoes 5-7 minutes on high heat. Cover & let stand.
2: Combine meat & onion in a casserole. Cook 2-3 minutes on high, stirring to break up the meat. Drain off any fat.
3: Stir in remaining ingredients & cook 3-5 minutes on high.
4: Scoop out potatoes & mash. Top the meat mixture with the mashed potatoes.
5: Sprinkle with paprika & cook uncovered 3-5 minutes on high heat.

per cup:

Dietary Fibre 1.8 Cholesterol 43 mg Carbohydrate 18 g
Total Fat 12 g Unsaturated Fat 5.6 Sodium 96 mg
Energy 249 kCal Protein 18 g Calcium 71 mg Iron 2.8 mg

MEATLESS SHEPHERD'S PIE

Use rehydrated T.V.P. (P.41) as a substitute for the meat in the above recipe.

LANCASHIRE HOT POT

A fancy name for "stew"... pictured on the front cover, this is good with salad & buns.

flour	¼ cup	50 ml
pepper	- to taste -	
beef chuck, cubed	½ lb.	250 g.
light beef bouillon cube	1	1
boiling water	1 cup	250 ml
Worcestershire sauce	½ tsp.	2 ml
potatoes, peeled & sliced	2	2
onion, chopped	½ cup	125 ml
carrot, sliced	1	1

1: Combine flour & pepper in a plastic bag & dredge the meat cubes in it.

2: Dissolve the bouillon cube in the boiling water & stir in the Worcestershire sauce.

3: Layer the vegetables & meat in a casserole dish.

4: Pour the bouillon mixture over top. Cover & bake for 5 minutes on high heat then for 20-30 minutes on medium (level 5, 50%, or half) heat. Allow 10 minutes "carry over cooking time".

per cup:

Dietary Fibre 1.3	Cholesterol 36 mg	Carbohydrate 14 g
Total Fat 8 g	Unsaturated Fat 2.9	Sodium 55 mg
Energy 213 kCal	Protein 20 g	Calcium 26 mg	Iron 2.1 mg

* You can add other vegetables to this, but remember... if you increase the quantities, you need to increase the cooking time.

MEATBALLS

Serve these on a bed of rice or with your favorite pasta.

lean ground beef	½ lb.	250 g.
minced onion	2 tsp.	10 ml
pepper	- to taste -	
parsley	1 tbsp.	15 ml
Worcestershire sauce	½ tsp.	2 ml
garlic powder	½ tsp.	2 ml
bread crumbs	¼ cup	50 ml
egg white	1	1

1: Mix all ingredients together & roll into meatballs.
2: Arrange meatballs on a microwave meat tray or pie plate. Cover with wax paper & cook 3-5 minutes on high heat.

MEATLOAF

Mix all ingredients as above & stuff into a small microwave safe loaf pan, small casserole, custard cups or microwave muffin cups. Cook as in "STEP 2".

BEEFBURGERS

Mix all ingredients as above, shape into patties & cook as in "STEP 2".

per meatball:

Dietary Fibre 0.1	Cholesterol 22 mg	Carbohydrate 5 g
Total Fat 6 g	Unsaturated Fat 2.6	Sodium 117 mg
Energy 151 kCal	Protein 16 g	Calcium 14 mg	Iron 1.7 mg

Variations :

Using the recipe on the opposite page, try the following variations....

TURKEY or CHICKEN BALLS , TURKEY or CHICKEN LOAF or TURKEY or CHICKEN BURGERS:
- substitute turkey or chicken for the ground beef & add 1 tsp. (5ml) soy sauce. For a nice "crunch" you could also add a few chopped water chestnuts.

TUNA BALLS, TUNA LOAF or TUNA BURGERS:
- substitute tuna (1: 6.5oz (184g)) can & ½ cup (125ml) chopped celery for the ground beef.

MEAT POCKETS:
- stuff chopped mushrooms , green pepper, spinach or bread stuffing into the center of any of the loaves or balls.

APPLESAUCE MEATBALLS :
- substitute ¼ cup (50ml) of applesauce or grated apple for the egg white...(it may be easier to buy applesauce in baby food jars for small amounts).

* Serve any of these with salsa sauce, yogurt sauce or Teriyaki sauce (P.62) or serve in pita pockets stuffed with lettuce, tomatoes, & yogurt sauce (P.62).

TERIYAKI SAUCE

Serve with chicken or meatballs (See P. 60-61)

soy sauce, low sodium	¼ cup	50 ml
crushed pineapple	½ cup	125 ml
dry sherry, optional	2 tbsp.	30 ml
ginger	¼ tsp.	1 ml
sugar	1 tbsp.	15 ml
cornstarch	1 tbsp.	15 ml
water	⅓ cup	75 ml

1: Combine all ingredients & cook on high heat 3-5 minutes, stirring twice.

per tbsp:

Dietary Fibre 0.1   Cholesterol 0 mg   Carbohydrate 2 g
Total Fat 0 g Unsaturated Fat 0.0 Sodium 87 mg
Energy 10 kCal Protein 0 g Calcium 1 mg Iron 0.1 mg

YOGURT SAUCE

Wonderful served with meat or tuna patties (See P. 60-61).

low fat yogurt	½ cup	125 ml
garlic powder	⅛ tsp.	.5 ml
mint leaves ⎫		
tarragon ⎬ suggested spices	½ tsp.	2 ml
dill weed ⎭		

1: Combine all ingredients & serve.

per tbsp:

Dietary Fibre 0.0   Cholesterol 1 mg   Carbohydrate 1 g
Total Fat 0 g Unsaturated Fat 0.1 Sodium 10 mg
Energy 10 kCal Protein 1 g Calcium 28 mg Iron 0.0 mg

GREAT BARBECUE SAUCE

ketchup, low sodium OR tomato sauce	½ cup	125 ml
garlic powder	½ tsp.	2 ml
brown sugar	2 tbsp.	30 ml
Worcestershire sauce	1 tbsp.	15 ml
lemon juice	1 tbsp.	15 ml
dry mustard	½ tsp.	2 ml
horseradish	½ tsp.	2 ml

1: Combine all ingredients & spoon over your favorite meat while it's cooking.

per tbsp:

Dietary Fibre 0.3   Cholesterol 0 mg   Carbohydrate 3 g
Total Fat 0 g   Unsaturated Fat 0.0   Sodium 17 mg
Energy 13 kCal   Protein 0 g   Calcium 4 mg   Iron 0.2 mg

LIGHT LUNCH

A light & fantastic treat!

tuna in water, drained	1 (6.5oz) can	1 (184g.) can
celery, sliced	¼ cup	50 ml
curry powder	1 tsp.	5 ml
light Miracle Whip	⅓ cup	75 ml
low fat milk	2 tbsp.	30 ml
papaya, peeled, sliced & scooped out	1	1

1: Mix all ingredients except the fruit. Serve in a papaya or cantelope cup on a bed of lettuce with one of our quick breads (P.112) Also try this with shrimp, crab meat or chicken.

per 4 oz. filling in papaya:

Dietary Fibre 0.7   Cholesterol 31 mg   Carbohydrate 7 g
Total Fat 8 g   Unsaturated Fat 6.6   Sodium 419 mg
Energy 174 kCal   Protein 17 g   Calcium 40 mg   Iron 0.7 mg

SEAFOOD:

Allow 4 min./lb. (8 min./kg.) for all your fish. It will flake with a fork when done. Don't forget that if you add stuffing or sauces, you'll have to increase the cooking time.

Cover your fish with plastic wrap for poaching, or wax paper for roasting.

For a nice steamed effect, wrap your fish in lettuce leaves.

You may also cook your fish in a brown paper bag! ... just make sure its not "recycled" paper... (if it is, it will be stamped on the bag). The fish skin will stick to the bag as its cooking.... when done, just peel off the bag & your fish is skinned!

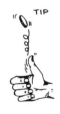

TIP

Leftovers can become "planned overs"... Your meals will be far more exciting if you freeze leftovers & pull them out at a later date ... when you won't think of them as "leftovers"!

TIP

Cooking is at its best when it involves other people ... invite your mate, roomate &/or friends to share.

SEAFOOD ROLLS

A nutritious recipe with many options.
See Photo P.64a

butter	1 tbsp.	15 ml
onion	2 tbsp.	30 ml
parsley	¼ cup	50 ml
dill leaves	1 tbsp.	15 ml
lemon juice	1 tbsp.	15 ml
fish fillets , (sole, cod etc)	1 lb.	½ kg

1: Combine butter & onion in a batter bowl. Cook on high heat, 30 sec - 1 min. or until onion is sautéed enough. Add remaining ingredients except the fish.

2: Spread the stuffing along each fillet, carefully roll up & secure with a toothpick.

3: Cover with plastic wrap & cook 4 minutes / lb. (500g)

4: Drain the juices & garnish with lemon slices & parsley.

per 3 oz. serving with 2 oz. stuffing:

*Dietary Fibre 0.3   Cholesterol 55 mg   Carbohydrate 1 g
Total Fat 4 g Unsaturated Fat 2.9 Sodium 121 mg
Energy 135 kCal Protein 22 g Calcium 27 mg Iron 1.1 mg*

Variations:

Stuff seafood rolls with shrimp, crab meat, bread stuffing etc.... & cook as above.

TIP

You can also use paper towel to wrap your fish in for easy removal of the skin. See P.64a

INDIVIDUAL SALMON LOAVES

low fat milk	½ cup	125 ml
flour	1 tbsp.	15 ml
frozen peas	½ cup	125 ml
canned salmon	1 (7¾ oz) can	1 (220 g.) can
mushrooms, chopped	¼ cup	50 ml
bread crumbs, optional	¼ cup	50 ml
onion powder	½ tsp.	2 ml
dill weed	½ tsp.	2 ml
egg	1	1

1: Combine milk, flour & mushrooms in a batter bowl & cook 1-3 minutes on high heat, stirring once or twice until thickened. Reserve half of this mixture for a topping.

2: Combine the other half of the mixture with the remaining ingredients.

3: Press into muffin cups, custard cups or ramekins. Cook on high heat, uncovered, for 2½ - 3½ minutes. Top with remaining mushroom sauce & heat the loaves another 45 seconds - 1 minute.

per muffin loaf:

Dietary Fibre 1.1   Cholesterol 77 mg   Carbohydrate 7 g
Total Fat 10 g   Unsaturated Fat 6.4   Sodium 266 mg
Energy 178 kCal   Protein 16 g   Calcium 145 mg   Iron 1.3 mg

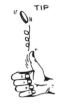 TIP

Make meatloaves or fish loaves in muffin cups or pans & freeze the extras.

SEAFOOD RATATOUILLE

Add seafood to this traditional vegetable dish, some whole wheat buns & you have a delicious meal!

halibut steaks OR any white fish	½ lb.	250 g.
onion, sliced	¼ cup	50 ml
zucchini, sliced	1 cup	250 ml
tomatoes, sliced	1	1
basil or thyme	½ tsp.	2 ml
pepper	— to taste —	
Parmesan cheese	— sprinkle —	

1: Cook fish in a shallow baking dish 2 minutes on high heat, covered with wax paper. (Fish cooks at 4 min./lb. (8.8 min./kg.).
2: Combine onion & zucchini in a pie plate. Cook on high heat 1½-2 minutes or until tender.
3: Stir in tomatoes & spices. Cook another 30 seconds - 1 minute on high heat.
4: Arrange cooked fish on a platter. Top with vegetable mixture & sprinkle with Parmesan cheese. Heat uncovered 20-30 seconds more if needed.

per 3oz. serving with 2oz. sauce:

Dietary Fibre 2.4 g Cholesterol 40 mg Carbohydrate 7 g
Total Fat 3 g Unsaturated Fat 2.1 g Sodium 78 mg
Energy 173 kCal Protein 28 g Calcium 82 mg Iron 1.7 mg

BLACKENED FISH

New Orleans style! This is best with a firm fish like snapper or cod. In a hurry?.... omit the seasonings & sprinkle the seafood with Cajun spice. Sensitive tummy?... omit the seasonings, cook the seafood as in "STEP 3" & serve with warmed "KIWI SAUCE" on opposite page.

fish fillets	½ lb.	250g.
chili powder	½ tsp.	2 ml
pepper	¼ tsp.	1 ml
cayenne	⅛ tsp.	.5 ml
paprika	1 tsp.	5 ml

1: Cut fish into two portions & place in a pie plate or microwave platter.
2: Combine the remaining ingredients & sprinkle both sides of the fish with it.
3: Cover with wax paper & cook 2-3 minutes on high heat. (4 min./lb. OR 8.8 min./kg.). Serve with "KIWI SAUCE" on opposite page.

per 3 oz. serving:

Dietary Fibre 0.4 g Cholesterol 47 mg   Carbohydrate 1 g
Total Fat 2 g Unsaturated Fat 1.0 g Sodium 86 mg
Energy 132 kCal Protein 26 g Calcium 45 mg Iron 0.6 mg

Remember... no need to grease dishes for microwave cooking, plus you can "sauté" without fat by just putting a lid on your dish or casserole.

KIWI SAUCE

This cold sauce is wonderful on seasoned fish or warm it up for 30 seconds-1 minute to serve on "naked" fillets.

Kiwi fruit	**2**	**2**
dried mint	1 tsp.	5 ml
onion powder	½ tsp.	2 ml
garlic powder	¼ tsp.	1 ml
sugar	½ tsp.	2 ml
white wine vinegar	1 tsp.	5 ml

1: Combine all ingredients & serve on or beside your seafood.

per tbsp:

Dietary Fibre 0.5   Cholesterol 0 mg   Carbohydrate 2 g
Total Fat 0 g Unsaturated Fat 0.0 Sodium 1 mg
Energy 10 kCal Protein 0 g Calcium 4 mg Iron 0.1 mg

Variation:

There are other fruits that also work well with this .... try it with pears, apples, grapes etc.

More than ½ your plate should be comprised of complex carbohydrates eg: whole grains, vegetables, beans, pasta, bread etc.

PASTA

Cooking pasta in the microwave oven will take just as long as doing it the conventional method ... BUT... you are saving energy with the microwave oven, "boil-overs" are so much easier to clean up, & many people prefer the texture of microwave pasta.

Follow the directions on the package for water & cooking times. You will find it faster to boil the water in your electric kettle. Cook pasta in a covered casserole on high heat. Allow 5 minutes "carry over cooking time" when it comes out of the oven. See Photo P.64a

<u>DRY PASTA</u> : requires 7-14 minutes in boiling water.

<u>FRESH PASTA</u> : requires 2-3 minutes in boiling water.

TIP
Warm dinner plates (no gold trim) by placing them "under" your casseroles while they're cooking... only do 2 plates at a time this way though.

TIP
When reheating food for two....put all the food on one plate, reheat & then divide in two ... that way you get to eat "together"!

"REAL" ITALIAN TOMATO SAUCE

A recipe shared with our daughter by a "real" Italian family .... Thanks Anna DeleCari! See Photo P.64a

Olive oil	1 tbsp.	15 ml
onion, chopped	½ cup	125 ml
tomatoes, fresh or canned	1(14oz.)can	1(398ml)can
tomato paste, optional	1-2 tbsp.	15-30ml
basil	½ tsp.	2 ml
oregano	½ tsp.	2 ml
garlic powder	¼ tsp.	1 ml

1: Combine onion & olive oil in a casserole. Sauté (cook) on high heat, 1-1½ minutes, uncovered.
2: Put tomatoes (fresh or canned) in the blender or food processor to break up. Leave the skin on fresh tomatoes, as this adds fibre to your diet.
3: Add all ingredients to the onion mixture. Stir tomato paste into to thicken if needed.
4: Simmer in a covered casserole, 6-10 minutes on high heat, stirring once.

per ¼ cup serving:

*Dietary Fibre 0.8 Cholesterol 0 mg Carbohydrate 4 g
Total Fat 2 g Unsaturated Fat 1.7 Sodium 92 mg
Energy 33 kCal Protein 1 g Calcium 20 mg Iron 0.5 mg*

* Read the labels on canned goods .... some are high in salt!

MACARONI & CHEESE

cooked pasta	2 cups	500 ml
cheese sauce :		
low fat milk	2 cups	500 ml
flour	2 tbsp.	30 ml
pepper	1/8 tsp.	.5 ml
soft margarine	1 tbsp.	15 ml
oregano	1 tsp.	5 ml
low fat cheese	3/4 cup	175 ml
tomatoes , chopped (optional)	1 cup	250 ml
bread crumbs , (optional)	1/2 cup	125 ml
soft margarine , (optional)	1 tsp.	5 ml

1: Combine milk, flour, pepper, margarine & oregano in a casserole. Heat 3-4 minutes on high, stirring 2-3 times to prevent lumping.

2: Stir cheese into the hot sauce. Let it stand for 5 minutes to allow the hot sauce to melt the cheese. Stir.

3: Mix in the cooked pasta & tomatoes .... (canned or fresh).

4: In a separate high heat resistant dish, combine the bread crumbs & 1 tsp. (5ml) of margarine. Heat on high for 45 seconds - 1 1/2 minutes, or until browned.

5: Sprinkle toasted bread crumbs over the casserole. Heat uncovered, 4-6 minutes on high heat.

per cup:

Dietary Fibre 0.8   Cholesterol 39 mg   Carbohydrate 24 g
Total Fat 6 g Unsaturated Fat 4.0 Sodium 475 mg
Energy 203 kCal Protein 12 g Calcium 305 mg Iron 1.5 mg

VEGETABLES

VEGETABLES:

COOKING GUIDE:

You will find a kitchen scale "invalu-able" with your vegetables!... "no guesswork"! The more you put into a microwave oven, the longer it takes & basically everything cooks by weight.

Allow 6 min./lb. (13 min./kg.) on high heat, with 5-10 minutes of "carry over cooking time" for your fresh or frozen vegetables. You will find this may vary slightly de-pending on whether you like your vegetables really crisp or soft .... & remember, if your casserole is really full, always stir half way through the cooking time.

ROOT VEGETABLES:

All vegetables that grow under ground (except onions), eg: potatoes, carrots, turnips etc., need a little moisture to soften them up. ¼" of water, chicken or beef stock or fruit juice etc. will do. Suggested cooking time:

1 cup (250ml) of root vegetable plus ¼" of liquid will take 2-3 minutes on high heat in a covered casserole. Let stand 5 min.

ABOVE · GROUND VEGETABLES:

Corn, broccoli, peas. cauliflower etc. don't need any added water, other than the water they've been washed in, as long as they're cooked covered.

* (2 exceptions to this rule are Brussels

sprouts & fresh beans.... they seem to need extra moisture while cooking, so treat them as root vegetables ... previous page).
Suggested cooking time:

1 cup (250 ml) of above-ground vegetable (except Brussels & fresh beans) will take 45 seconds-1½minute on high heat in a covered casserole.

CANNED VEGETABLES:

These really just need heating, so drain & allow 1-2 minutes/cup on high heat.

BLANCHING VEGETABLES:

No more pots of boiling water in a hot kitchen !! Grab an iced tea & relax ... it's a piece of cake! Prepare vegetables as for cooking (previous page). Allow 3 min./lb. or 6½ min./kg. on high heat. Plunge into ice water, drain, place in freezer bags & VOILÀ!

BAKED POTATO, SQUASH, TURNIP, OR SWEET POTATO:

Wash, pierce as for conventional cooking & allow 6 min./lb. or 13 min./kg. on high heat. A medium potato will take 4-6 min. on high heat & 5 minutes standing time. A larger, more dense vegetable like a turnip will need more time... add 4-8 minutes or as needed to cook.

CORN ON THE COB:

Cook in the husk or in an oblong pan covered with plastic wrap, turning back a corner to allow a steam vent. Allow about 2-3 minutes / cob on high heat.

ASPARAGUS:

A special vegetable due to its size .... most people overcook it! Wrap it in paper towel & run the paper towel under water to keep the vegetable moist (or... start with the stems & add the tips half way through the cooking). Asparagus for 1 or 2 will want about 45 sec. - 1½ min. If you're cooking it in a casserole for guests, allow 6 min./lb. or 13 min./kg. as for other above-ground vegetables. See Photo P. 80a

Here are some easy additions to make vegetables "Come Alive":

 TIP

1) Before Cooking Add:
- a little chopped red or green pepper
- sliced mushrooms
- chopped celery or onion
- ¼ - ½ tsp. (1-2 ml) basil, thyme or tarragon
- or combine vegetables

2) After Cooking:
- sprinkle with cheese & melt.
- sprinkle with dry bread/cracker crumbs
- sprinkle with parsley
- sprinkle cinnamon on squash

VEGETABLE TOSS

Choose your vegetables & using the vegetable cooking guide (P. 74-76) start with the more dense vegetables ... eg: carrots, onion & broccoli stalks ... & end with mushrooms .... adding different vegetables during the cooking process. I usually cook the vegetables covered & always on high heat. For this type of dish I don't always give the vegetables 6 min./lb. (13 min./kg.), as they are nicer if they're a little more crunchy....

carrot, sliced	½ cup	125 ml
broccoli stalks, peeled & sliced	½ cup	125 ml
cauliflower	½ cup	125 ml
broccoli flowerettes	½ cup	125 ml
mushrooms OR tomato wedges	½ cup	125 ml
spices		– sprinkle –

1: Cook carrots & broccoli stalks 45 sec.-1min. on high heat in a covered casserole. (I don't add water to these).

2: Stir in cauliflower. Cook another 30 sec.-1min.

3: Stir in broccoli flowerettes, mushrooms &/or tomatoes. Cook another 30 sec-1min.

4: Serve as is or add a dab of margarine &/or basil, thyme or dill weed.

per cup:

Dietary Fibre 4.3 g Cholesterol 0 mg Carbohydrate 13 g
Total Fat 1 g Unsaturated Fat 0.3 g Sodium 46 mg
Energy 62 kCal Protein 4 g Calcium 65 mg Iron 1.7 mg

CHINESE STIR FRY

soy sauce, low sodium	2 tsp.	10 ml
brown sugar	1½ tsp.	7 ml
olive oil	1 tsp.	5 ml
ginger, optional	- pinch -	

1: Combine all ingredients & toss with cooked vegetables (previous page).

per ½ recipe with 1 cup vegetables:

Dietary Fibre 4.3 g Cholesterol 0 mg Carbohydrate 16 g
Total Fat 3 g Unsaturated Fat 2.2 g Sodium 216 mg
Energy 94 kCal Protein 5 g Calcium 68 mg Iron 1.8 mg

SWEDISH BAKED POTATOES

potatoes, peeled & oval-shaped	1-2	1-2
olive oil	brush with	
Parmesan cheese	sprinkle with	
dry bread crumbs, (or cracker)		

1: Cut potatoes in slices along the width, BUT not all the way through.
2: Brush with olive oil & arrange in a covered casserole, cut side down.
3: Cook 2-3 min. on high heat, turning over & basting half way through.
4: Sprinkle with cheese & crumbs, now with the sliced side up.
5: Cover with wax paper & cook another 2-3 min. on high heat. Allow 5 min. "carry over cooking time" & serve.

per potato:

Dietary Fibre 1.5 g Cholesterol 1 mg Carbohydrate 18 g
Total Fat 3 g Unsaturated Fat 2.0 g Sodium 29 mg
Energy 105 kCal Protein 2 g Calcium 19 mg Iron 0.7 mg

QUICK SCALLOPED POTATOES

See Photo P.80a

potatoes, sliced	2	2
onions, sliced	½ cup	125 ml
low fat milk	1 cup	250 ml
flour	2 tbsp.	25 ml
pepper	- to taste -	
dry mustard	¼ tsp.	1 ml
paprika	- sprinkle -	

1: Slice potatoes (I leave the peel on) & the onions. Combine in a covered casserole with enough milk to cover the bottom of the dish (¼")... always allow this much liquid for root vegetables.

2: Cook 6-10 minutes on high heat.

3: Drain the milk off the potatoes into a measuring cup. Top it up with more milk to make 1 cup (250ml.) Whisk in flour, pepper & mustard. Heat 3·4 minutes on high heat until thickened, stirring twice.

4: Combine sauce with cooked potato mixture. Sprinkle liberally with paprika, cover with wax paper & bake 3-5 minutes on high heat.

per ½ cup serving:

Dietary Fibre 1.2   Cholesterol 1 mg   Carbohydrate 16 g
Total Fat 0 g   Unsaturated Fat 0.1   Sodium 33 mg
Energy 81 kCal   Protein 4 g   Calcium 81 mg   Iron 0.6 mg

Variation:

"Au Gratin": top with ½ cup (125ml) of low fat cheese in the last 30 seconds of the cooking time.

POTATO WEDGES

potatoes	1-2	1-2
olive oil	1-2 tsp.	5-10 ml
basil OR thyme	1-2 tsp.	5-10 ml
Parmesan cheese, optional	1-2 tsp.	5-10 ml
salt & pepper, optional	- to taste -	

1: Slice potatoes into wedges (I leave the skin on).
2: Toss with oil, spice or other options.
3: Cover with wax paper & allow 7 min./lb. or 14 min./kg. on high heat, rearranging half way through the cooking time.

* These take a little longer per lb.(kg.) than other potatoes because they do not have the added heat of being steamed!

   I potato will take about 4-5 minutes.
   2 potatoes will take about 6-7 minutes.

per potato:

> *Dietary Fibre 1.6 g Cholesterol 0 mg Carbohydrate 18 g*
> *Total Fat 5 g Unsaturated Fat 3.9 g Sodium 6 mg*
> *Energy 120 kCal Protein 2 g Calcium 15 mg Iron 0.9 mg*

CRUMB COATED POTATOES

Another recipe with endless options....
why not toss the potatoes in melted butter instead of the oil, & then in seasoned bread crumbs, Shake 'n Bake, or cracker crumbs & Parmesan cheese.

LAMB CHOPS P. 40
SCALLOPED POTATOES P. 79
ASPARAGUS P. 76

ROAST POTATOES

Toss potato wedges, cubes or slices in a mixture of:

olive oil	1 tsp. (5ml) per potato
low sodium beef stock	1 tsp. (5ml) per potato
pepper	to taste
other spices if desired	

1: Cook as for "Potato Wedges" on previous page.

LEMON POTATOES

Toss potato wedges, cubes or slices in a mixture of:

olive oil OR melted butter (margarine)	1 tsp (5ml) per potato
lemon juice	1 tsp. (5ml) per potato
low sodium chicken stock	1 tsp. (5ml) per potato
tarragon, basil or thyme	½ tsp. (2ml) per potato

1: Cook as for "Potato Wedges" on previous page.

whenever possible, leave the skin on your vegetables ....
eg: potatoes, carrots, beets etc.

PARSLIED POTATOES

1: Bake potato (es) whole or cut up with ¼" water on the bottom of the dish.... (See Vegetable Cooking Guide P. 74-75). Let stand 5 minutes.

2: Drain if necessary, then toss with melted butter (or soft margarine) & chopped parsley.

per potato:

Dietary Fibre 1.6 g Cholesterol 0 mg   Carbohydrate 18 g
Total Fat 2 g Unsaturated Fat 1.6 g Sodium 24 mg
Energy 99 kCal Protein   2 g Calcium 8 mg Iron 1.0 mg

Variations:

Use dill weed instead of parsley when serving with fish, tarragon instead of parsley when serving with chicken, or just sprinkle with Parmesan cheese for a nice change.

MASHED POTATOES

1: Bake potato (es) whole or peel & cut up in a casserole with ¼" of water in the bottom of the dish... (See Vegetable Cooking Guide P. 74-75). Let stand 5 min.

2: Drain if necessary, then mash adding a little soft margarine & low fat milk (or vegetable water) as needed. A sprinkle of pepper &/or garlic powder is also good.

per ½ cup:

Dietary Fibre 1.5 g Cholesterol 0 mg   Carbohydrate 18 g
Total Fat 2 g Unsaturated Fat 1.6 g Sodium 27 mg
Energy 99 kCal Protein 2 g Calcium 17 mg Iron 1.0 mg

CARROTS AU GRATIN

The crumb topping on this dish makes a tasty topping for any casserole.

carrots, sliced	1½ cups	375 ml
green pepper, chopped	2 tbsp.	30 ml
onion, chopped	1 tbsp.	15 ml
water		

1: Arrange the ingredients in a covered casserole & add enough water to cover the bottom of the dish by ¼".
2: Cook 2½ - 3½ minutes on high heat. Let stand 5 minutes & drain.

cracker or bread crumbs	¼ cup	50 ml
soft margarine	1 tbsp.	15 ml
Parmesan cheese	1 tbsp.	15 ml

1: Combine these three ingredients in a small casserole.
2: Cook 45 seconds - 1½ minutes on high heat until toasted, then sprinkle over cooked carrots above.

per ½ cup serving:

*Dietary Fibre 2.1   Cholesterol 2 mg   Carbohydrate 16 g
Total Fat 5 g Unsaturated Fat 3.9 Sodium 172 mg
Energy 121 kCal Protein   3 g Calcium 59 mg   Iron 1.5 mg*

Variation:

Chopped celery is also good in this recipe.

SCALLOPED CABBAGE

This is also great with spinach, peas, broccoli, carrots etc.

cabbage, shredded	4 cups	1 L
mozarella cheese; low fat, grated	¼ cup	50 ml
milk	½ cup	125 ml
flour	1 tbsp.	15 ml
pepper	- to taste -	
prepared mustard	1 tsp.	5 ml
sugar	½ tsp.	2 ml
dry bread crumbs, optional	¼ cup	50 ml

1: Cook cabbage for 5-6 minutes on high heat, in a covered casserole.
2: Combine milk, flour, pepper, mustard & sugar in a small bowl. Cook on high heat for 1½-2 minutes, stirring every 30 seconds until thickened.
3: Layer half of the cabbage in a small casserole. Top with grated cheese then cover with the rest of the cabbage.
4: Pour the sauce over the cabbage casserole, top with bread crumbs & cook 1-2 minutes, uncovered, on high heat.

per ½ cup serving:

*Dietary Fibre 2.4 Cholesterol 7 mg Carbohydrate 12 g
Total Fat 2 g Unsaturated Fat 0.9 Sodium 121 mg
Energy 89 kCal Protein 6 g Calcium 190 mg Iron 0.9 mg*

* This recipe is really nice stuffed in green pepper, scooped out tomato or onion cups See photo P. 64a

SIMPLE RATATOUILLE

This is wonderful with seafood,
Couscous P.86 & Thai Turkey Balls P.57

tomatoes , cut in wedges	1-2	1-2
small zucchini, sliced	1	1
onion, sliced	½ cup	125 ml
red & green peppers , sliced	½ cup (ea)	125 ml(ea)
garlic , powder or clove	⅛ tsp.	.5 ml

1: Sauté (cook) onion & garlic in a covered casserole 45 sec- 1min. on high heat.
2: Stir in peppers & zucchini. Cook un-covered another 2-3 minutes on high heat.
3: Stir in tomato wedges & cook 1-2 min. more or until vegetables are cooked to taste.

per ½ cup serving:

Dietary Fibre 1.8   Cholesterol 0 mg   Carbohydrate 6 g
Total Fat 0 g Unsaturated Fat 0.2 Sodium   7 mg
Energy 29 kCal   Protein   1 g Calcium 12 mg Iron 0.5 mg

Use less fats... most micro-wave dishes can do without the butter or fat.

Enjoy your meals ..... don't eat over the sink , on the run or from a package ! Also ... share your meals with a friend!

COUSCOUS

Couscous is made from semolina wheat. It is a very popular dish from Morocco & is now working its way into our kitchens! It's a healthy addition to any meal .... served with Simple Ratatouille P. 85 & Thai Turkey Balls P. 57 , it is a family favorite.

onion, chopped	¼ cup	50 ml
garlic powder	⅛ tsp.	.5 ml
cumin	1 tsp.	5 ml
curry powder	1 tsp.	5 ml
couscous	½ cup	125 ml
chicken stock , low sodium OR tomato juice	1 cup	250 ml
pepper	– to taste –	

1: Sauté (cook) onion, garlic, cumin & curry in a covered casserole, 45 sec. - 1 min. on high heat.
2: Add remaining ingredients & cook 5 minutes , covered, on high heat. Let stand 5 minutes.

per ½ cup serving:

Dietary Fibre 0.7   Cholesterol 1 mg   Carbohydrate 25 g
Total Fat 4 g Unsaturated Fat 0.9 Sodium   5 mg
Energy 162 kCal Protein   7 g Calcium 31 mg Iron 1.2 mg

TIP

Freeze leftover meat or vegetable stock in ice cube trays & then store in freezer bags for later use in your recipes.

RICE

Try Basmati rice, barley or orzo (a rice-shaped pasta) in these recipes.

A. <u>BASIC LONG GRAIN RICE</u>:
   · you can use wild rice too!

long grain rice	½ cup	125 ml
water	1 cup	250 ml

1. Combine rice & water in a covered casserole. Cook 6-7 minutes on high heat. Let stand 5-10 minutes or until water is absorbed.

* Remember how important "carry-over cooking time" is ?.... well, your rice may not be done after 7 minutes, BUT..... it will be done after standing time.

* A little more liquid can be added near the end of the cooking time if the rice is not tender & nearly dry.

* Many types of rice need to be washed before cooking.

Remember... there is no "scorching" in the microwave oven as there is no direct heat.

TIP

B. <u>BASIC MINUTE RICE</u>:

water	½ cup	125 ml
minute rice	½ cup	125 ml

1: Bring water to a boil in a covered casserole (about 1-2 minutes on high heat).
2: Add rice & let stand covered, 5-7 min.

C. <u>BASIC BROWN RICE</u>:
- brown rice takes a long time to cook
in the microwave oven, just as it does
conventionally!

water	1¼ cups	300 ml
brown rice	½ cup	125 ml

1: Combine water & rice in a covered casserole, cook 3 minutes on high heat,
then 12 minutes on power level 3 or defrost. Let stand 10 minutes "carry over
cooking time".

TIP

Freeze leftover meat or vegetable
stock for use later to enhance
the flavor of rice or other recipes
calling for water.

RICE PILAF

almonds	¼ cup	50 ml
soft margarine	1 tbsp.	15 ml
rice, white or brown	½ cup	125 ml
carrot, thinly sliced	½ cup	125 ml
celery, thinly sliced	½ cup	125 ml
soy sauce, low sodium	1 tbsp.	15 ml
beef stock, low sodium	1 tbsp.	15 ml
water	1 cup	250 ml

1: Combine almonds & margarine in a high heat resistant dish. Cook uncovered, 2-4 minutes on high heat, stirring twice, until browned. Set aside.

2: Combine the remaining ingredients in a covered casserole. Cook 6 minutes on high heat. Let stand 10 minutes. (If the mixture wants to boil over... turn the heat down).

3: Just before serving, stir in the toasted almonds.

per ½ cup serving:

Dietary Fibre 2.4   Cholesterol 0 mg   Carbohydrate 18 g
Total Fat 8 g Unsaturated Fat 6.4 Sodium 324 mg
Energy 156 kCal Protein 4 g Calcium 48 mg Iron 1.3 mg

* Remember... regular brown rice always takes longer to cook (see previous page).

Variations:

-try other vegetables in this ... if using broccoli or mushroom pieces, add near the end of the cooking time.

- also try barley instead of rice in this....

RICE ... more variations :

Instead of water, try cooking your rice in the following :

1: <u>TOMATO RICE</u> .... use tomato juice.

2: <u>BEEF RICE</u> .... use low sodium beef stock.

3: <u>CHICKEN RICE</u> .... use low sodium chicken stock.

4: <u>VEGETABLE PILAF</u> .... add vegetables, eg: carrot, celery, onion

5: <u>ORANGE RICE</u> .... use ¼ cup (50 ml) of orange juice & ¾ cup (75 ml) of water.

TIP

You can also add almonds & /or raisins to any of the above variations.

When shopping, check all your labels ... oil is "fat" even if it has no cholesterol.

DESSERTS

BAKED APPLES

So easy & this can cook while you're eating dinner!

apples	as needed	as needed
brown sugar	1 tbsp./apple	15 ml/apple
cinnamon	Sprinkle	Sprinkle
butter	1 tsp./apple	5 ml/apple

1: Core apples & peel totally or just around the centre. Slice or leave whole.

2: Combine sugar, cinnamon & butter. Sprinkle mixture on each apple.

3: Cook covered, on high heat as follows:

1 apple	-	2-2½ minutes
2 apples	-	3-3½ minutes
3 apples	-	4-4½ minutes
4 apples	-	5-5½ minutes

per apple:

Dietary Fibre 1.7 g Cholesterol 0 mg   Carbohydrate 24 g
Total Fat 4 g Unsaturated Fat 3.1 g Sodium 38 mg
Energy 126 kCal Protein   0 g Calcium 23 mg Iron 1.2 mg

Replace up to ½ the oil in baked goods with applesauce or low fat yogurt.

Low fat cottage cheese can be puréed & used in recipes calling for sour cream or as a low calorie dip.

APPLESAUCE

1: Peel & chop apples or wash & chop finely in a food processor..... if you leave the skin on to obtain fibre, you'll want it chopped into small bits for easy digestion.

2: Cook apples in a covered casserole at 6 min./lb. (13 min./kg.) on high heat.... no need to add water. See suggested times below.

HOT APPLE SLICES

Hot apple slices make a tasty garnish for meat dishes.

1: Arrange sliced apples on a bread & butter plate or small flat dish.

2: Cover & cook on high heat ... slices will hold their shape.... & remember you can use an inverted plate, lid or plastic wrap as your cover.

Cooking times: (6 min./lb. or 13 min./kg.)

1 apple	-	2-2½ minutes
2 apples	-	3-3½ minutes
3 apples	-	4-4½ minutes
4 apples	-	5-5½ minutes

per apple:

Dietary Fibre 1.1 g	Cholesterol 0 mg	Carbohydrate 9 g
Total Fat 0 g	Unsaturated Fat 0.1 g	Sodium 0 mg
Energy 35 kCal	Protein 0 g	Calcium 4 mg Iron 0.1 mg

BAKED FRUIT

A wonderful, light dessert. Use pears, peaches, nectarines, apples or a combination using strawberries, blueberries, raspberries etc. for colour.

fruit, fresh or canned	2	2
orange juice	¼ cup	50ml
orange peel	¼ tsp.	1 ml
water	¼ cup	50ml
cinnamon	⅛ tsp.	.5 ml
cornstarch	2 tsp.	10 ml
almonds	¼ cup	50 ml
low fat yogurt, optional	¼ cup	50 ml

1: Peel fruit & cut lengthwise or leave whole. Arrange cut side up in a dish.
2: Combine all ingredients, except the fruit & almonds, in a batter bowl. Thicken 1-2 minutes on high heat, stirring once or twice. Pour over fruit.
3: Toast almonds in a high heat resistant dish (ie: glass pie plate). Allow 1-2 minutes on high heat, stirring 2-3 times to make sure they don't burn.
4: Cover fruit with wax paper & cook 3-4 minutes on high heat (canned fruit will need less time).
5: Top fruit with low fat yogurt & toasted almonds... & ... shaved chocolate if desired!

per pear, peach etc:

Dietary Fibre 5.6 g	Cholesterol 0 mg	Carbohydrate 30 g
Total Fat 9 g	Unsaturated Fat 7.5 g	Sodium 2 mg
Energy 201 kCal	Protein 4 g	Calcium 64 mg Iron 1.1 mg

FRUIT CRISP

The best yet! Great served with ice cream, cream or yogurt.

berries , strawberries, raspberries etc.	½ cup	125 ml
nectarine or peach , sliced	1	1
apples , sliced	2	2
white sugar	2 tbsp.	30 ml
flour	1 tbsp.	15 ml
cinnamon	¼ tsp.	1 ml
butter	1 tsp.	5 ml
lemon juice	1 tbsp.	15 ml
brown sugar	½ cup	125 ml
flour or oatmeal	½ cup	125 ml
butter	3 tbsp.	50 ml
walnuts, pecans or almonds	¼ cup	50 ml

1: Place fruit in a small casserole, custard cups or ramekins.
2: Mix together the next 5 ingredients, & blend well with the fruit.
3: Mix together the next 3 ingredients & crumble over the fruit mixture, sprinkle with chopped nuts & then pat down with wax paper or the back of a spoon.
4: Cook uncovered, 6-7 minutes on high heat ...(this can cook while you're eating dinner)!

per ½ cup serving:
Dietary Fibre 2.5 g Cholesterol 0 mg Carbohydrate 52 g
Total Fat 6 g Unsaturated Fat 4.6 g Sodium 18 mg
Energy 263 kCal Protein 3 g Calcium 37 mg Iron 1.6 mg

Variation: for Apple Crisp use 3 apples & omit the other fruits.

DESSERTS 95

CAKES

There are three very important things to know about microwaving cakes.....

1: <u>USE MEDIUM - SIZED EGGS</u>:
They are smaller than large or farm fresh eggs, & it's a good way to adjust the moisture. Less moisture is needed in a microwave cake because cooking time is shorter, the oven isn't hot so... you lose less to evaporation.

2: <u>DON'T OVER-MIX</u>:
I use a whisk or beat with a mixer or food processor for a short time. Micro-wave cakes don't need as much mixing time as cakes for the regular oven.... as a matter of fact, I find if you do over-mix them, they tend to be tough or chewy!

3: <u>LET THE BATTER SIT 5 MINUTES</u>:
Cake or muffins bake so fast in the microwave oven that often the leaven-ing agent doesn't get much time. So, let the batter sit, let the bubbles start forming & the batter thicken...... & it will have a much nicer texture.

You don't have to grease pans going into the microwave oven because there is no hot air to "bake" foods. Also, your foods don't get a crust in the microwave oven because the air is moist & the edges don't dry (crust).... some of you could argue this when you have overcooked something & it turns to "ROCK"... but that's another story!! For this reason, (no crust), I like to line cake pans with wax paper ... it helps your cakes come out of the pans in one piece.

A cake from the microwave oven, just like a cake from the regular oven, should sit in the pan 5-10 minutes after cooking, before turning it out. (It is far too fragile when it first comes out).

LOW CHOLESTEROL CAKE:

You can use 2 egg whites in place of 1 whole egg... (the cholesterol is in the yolk). You can also use egg substitute, (See P. 121).

TROUBLE BAKING A CAKE?

1: Make sure to use medium eggs.
2: Always let the batter sit for 5 min.
3: Try elevating the cake on an upside-down casserole or muffin pan during baking.
4: Cakes bake better in plastic rather than glassware ... the glass seems to take heat away from the batter.

LOW FAT CHOCOLATE CAKE

Minus the eggs & the milk, this is a low fat, quick & easy dessert.

flour	1½ cups	375 ml
sugar	1 cup	250 ml
baking powder (see TIP below)	1 tsp.	5 ml
baking soda	1 tsp.	5 ml
cocoa	¼ cup	50 ml
soft margarine	¼ cup	50 ml
vinegar	1 tbsp.	15 ml
vanilla	2 tsp.	10 ml
warm water	1 cup	250 ml

1: Combine the first 5 ingredients.
2: Whisk together the remaining ingredients in a separate bowl.
3: Combine both mixtures, just until mixed.
4: Let the batter sit for 5 minutes to allow the leavening agent to start working.
5: Pour the mixture into an 8" (20 cm) square, round or bundt pan.
6: Cook 6-7 minutes on high heat or until a toothpick comes out clean.

per 2"x 2" slice:

Dietary Fibre 1.2 g	Cholesterol 0 mg	Carbohydrate 23 g
Total Fat 3 g	Unsaturated Fat 2.5 g	Sodium 54 mg
Energy 125 kCal	Protein 2 g	Calcium 7 mg Iron 1.0 mg

See P. 22 to make your own Sodium-free Baking Powder.

FEATHER CAKE

This is low fat & delicious topped with a cake sauce (P.105), dessert topping (P.106) or just with fresh fruit.

flour	1 cup	250 ml
sugar	¾ cup	175 ml
baking powder (See Tip P.98)	2 tsp.	10 ml
soft margarine	¼ cup	50 ml
low fat milk	½ cup	125 ml
vanilla OR	½ tsp.	2 ml
almond flavoring	⅛ tsp.	.5 ml
egg whites	2 medium	2 medium

1: Combine all ingredients, except the egg whites, in a mixing bowl. Mix well.
2: Beat egg whites.
3: Fold beaten egg whites into the cake mixture & mix well. Let stand 5 min.
4: Line the bottom of an 8"(20cm) cake pan with wax paper ... no need to grease the pan.
5: Pour batter into the pan & cook 4-4½ minutes on high heat or until a toothpick comes out clean. Let stand 5-10 minutes before turning out.

per 2"x2" slice:

Dietary Fibre 0.3 g Cholesterol 0 mg   Carbohydrate 16 g
Total Fat 3 g Unsaturated Fat 2.4 g Sodium 74 mg
Energy 98 kCal Protein 2 g Calcium 15 mg Iron 0.7 mg

* Remember, cakes take less time in the microwave oven so don't over heat or they'll be tough & chewy.

SNACK 'N CAKE

This recipe calls for ½ cup (125ml) of "mash" (applesauce, carrot, apricot, banana, pumpkin, shredded zucchini etc.....). Purée your own or shop the baby food section of your grocery store ... they can supply you with an endless array of flavors & in small quantities!

raisins	½ cup	125 ml
water	1 cup	250 ml
vegetable oil	⅓ cup	75 ml
"mash"	½ cup	125 ml
eggs, medium	2	2
milk	3 tbsp.	50 ml
sugar	⅔ cup	150 ml
flour	1 cup	250 ml
baking soda	1 tsp.	5 ml
cinnamon	½ tsp.	2 ml
nutmeg	¼ tsp.	1 ml
cloves	¼ tsp.	1 ml

1: Combine the raisins & water in a small bowl & cook 1½ minutes on high heat. Let stand 3-5 minutes to plump the raisins. Drain & set aside on paper towel to drain again. (If you would rather not have raisins in this recipe, just omit them & the water!)

2: Beat together the eggs, milk & sugar.

3: Mix in the remaining ingredients, including the raisins. Do not over-mix the cake or it will be chewy.

4: Let the batter sit for about 5 minutes to allow the leavening agent to start working.

5: Line a bundt pan or 8"(20cm) cake pan with wax paper....(there's no need to grease a pan for the microwave oven as there is no dry heat to bake things on!)

6: Pour the batter into the pan & bake for 4 minutes on high heat. Test with a toothpick for doneness.

per 2" x 2" slice:

Dietary Fibre 0.4 g	*Cholesterol 27 mg*	*Carbohydrate 14 g*
Total Fat 5 g	*Unsaturated Fat 4.4 g*	*Sodium 21 mg*
Energy 104 kCal	*Protein 1 g*	*Calcium 11 mg* *Iron 0.3 mg*

Variation:

Use egg substitute (See P. 121) or use 4 egg whites to cut the cholesterol.

Anything that comes out of the microwave oven "Dry, Hard or Rubbery" has been overcooked!

TIP

Always try to use low fat dairy products: (Skim or 1%) (See Tip P. 21).

BASIC WHITE CAKE

Serve these cakes with fruit, frosting or sauces (See P. 105-106).

sugar	½ cup	125 ml
egg, medium	1	1
milk	½ cup	125 ml
soft margarine	¼ cup	50 ml
vanilla	½ tsp.	2 ml
flour	1 cup	250 ml
baking powder (See Tip P.98)	2 tsp.	10 ml

1: Combine the first 5 ingredients & mix well.
2: Mix in the flour & baking powder ... try not to "over mix" or it will be tough or chewy!
3: Let the batter sit for 5 minutes to allow the leavening agent to start working.
4: Line the bottom of an 8" (20cm) square, round or bundt pan with wax paper .... no need to grease pans that go into the microwave oven.
5: Pour the batter into the pan & bake 4-5 minutes on high heat, or until a toothpick comes out clean.

per 2"x2" slice:

Dietary Fibre 0.3 g   Cholesterol 14 mg   Carbohydrate 13 g
Total Fat 3 g   Unsaturated Fat 2.6 g   Sodium 70 mg
Energy 88 kCal   Protein 1 g   Calcium 16 mg   Iron 0.7 mg

When baking, you can use 2 egg whites in place of 1 egg in your recipes ... it is the yolk that is high in cholesterol.

BASIC CHOCOLATE CAKE

soft margarine	¼ cup	50 ml
cocoa	1 tbsp.	15 ml
chocolate chips, optional	¼ cup	50 ml

1: Combine margarine with "Step 1" (previous page).
2: Mix cocoa & chips with the dry ingredients & bake as for "White Cake" (previous page).

LEMON CAKE

lemon juice (or concentrate)	¼ cup	50 ml
water	¼ cup	50 ml
lemon peel	1 tsp.	5 ml

1: Substitute lemon juice & water for the milk in the "White Cake" recipe (previous page). Add lemon peel & bake as directed.

ORANGE CAKE

orange juice	½ cup	125 ml
orange peel	1 tsp.	5 ml

1: Substitute orange juice for the milk in the "White Cake" recipe (previous page). Add orange peel & bake as directed.

Remember, you don't have to grease dishes for microwave cooking.

POPPY SEED CAKE

| poppy seed | 2 tbsp. | 30 ml |
| cherries , chopped | ¼ cup | 50 ml |

1: Following the "White Cake" recipe (P. 102) soak the poppy seed in the milk first, for about 30 minutes.

2: Mix into the cake , stir in the cherries & bake as directed Steps 1-5 (P.102).

STEWED RHUBARB

rhubarb , sliced	2 cups	500 ml
cornstarch	1 tbsp.	15 ml
orange peel, grated	1 tbsp.	15 ml
nutmeg	⅛ tsp	.5 ml
sugar	½ cup	125 ml
orange juice	¼ cup	50 ml

1: Combine all the ingredients in a 1 qt (1L) casserole.

2: Cook covered , 4-5 minutes on high heat. Let stand 5-10 minutes.

per ½ cup serving :

Dietary Fibre 2.0   Cholesterol 0 mg   Carbohydrate 26 g
Total Fat 0 g Unsaturated Fat 0.0 Sodium   2 mg
Energy 101 kCal Protein   1 g Calcium 181 mg Iron 0.3 mg

 TIP Foods won't "scorch" & you don't have to stir things as often because there is no "direct" heat in a microwave. The heat comes in on all sides, top & bottom.

VANILLA SAUCE

sugar	⅓ cup	175 ml
milk	1 cup	250 ml
soft margarine	¼ cup	50 ml
cornstarch	1 tbsp.	15 ml
vanilla	1 tsp.	5 ml

1: Whisk the first four ingredients together in a batter bowl.
2: Cook uncovered, 4-5 minutes on high heat, until thickened.
3: Stir in vanilla & serve sauce over slices of cake &/or fruit.

per tbsp:

Dietary Fibre 0.0   Cholesterol 0 mg   Carbohydrate 5 g
Total Fat 1 g Unsaturated Fat 1.2 Sodium 17 mg
Energy 36 kCal Protein 0 g Calcium 10 mg Iron 0.2 mg

CHOCOLATE SAUCE

1: Whisk ¼ cup (50ml) of cocoa into the "Vanilla Sauce" recipe above. Cook as directed.

RASPBERRY SAUCE

1: Following "Vanilla Sauce" recipe above, substitute 1 cup (250ml) of raspberry purée in water, in place of the milk. This is nice with white or chocolate cake.

LEMON SAUCE

1. Following "Vanilla Sauce" recipe (previous page), substitute ¼ cup (50ml) of lemon juice & ¾ cup (175ml) of water in place of the milk. Also omit the vanilla.

LOW FAT DESSERT TOPPING

1. Whip ⅔ cup (150ml) of evaporated skim milk & sweeten with 1 tsp. (5ml) of sugar or honey & 1 tsp. (5ml) of vanilla.

* The milk, bowl & beaters should be well chilled before beating.

per tbsp:

Dietary Fibre 0.0   Cholesterol 0 mg   Carbohydrate 2 g
Total Fat 0 g Unsaturated Fat 0.0 Sodium 16 mg
Energy 14 kCal Protein 1 g Calcium 41 mg Iron 0.0 mg

Try using less fats in your cooking: Most microwave dishes can do without butter or fat. The only exception is in "baking", but the fat in baking can be reduced by replacing up to "½" with applesauce or plain yogurt.

You can also use low fat yogurt to make low fat salad dressings, fruit dip or to dilute mayonnaise.

CHOCOLATE FUDGE PUDDING

flour	½ cup	125 ml
baking powder	1 tsp.	5 ml
sugar	⅓ cup	75 ml
cocoa	1 tbsp.	15 ml
vegetable oil	1 tbsp.	15 ml
vanilla	½ tsp.	2 ml
milk	¼ cup	50 ml

1: Mix together the first four ingredients.
2: Stir in the remaining ingredients, just until blended.
3: Pour into a small casserole or two dessert cups.
4: Top with the following mixture:

brown sugar	⅓ cup	75 ml
cocoa	2 tbsp.	25 ml
chopped nuts, optional	¼ cup	50 ml

5: Pour 1 cup (250 ml) of boiling water or hot coffee over the pudding mixture.
6: Cover with wax paper & cook 3-4 minutes on high heat.

per ½ cup serving:

Dietary Fibre 2.5 Cholesterol 1 mg Carbohydrate 58 g
Total Fat 8 g Unsaturated Fat 6.7 Sodium 156 mg
Energy 321 kCal Protein 5 g Calcium 59 mg Iron 1.4 mg

Variation:
For a "rich" treat .... substitute chocolate chips for chopped nuts!

REFRIGERATOR BRAN MUFFINS

This recipe makes about 10 muffins &
the batter will keep 4-5 weeks in the fridge!

All Bran cereal or bran	1½ cups	425 ml
water	½ cup	125 ml
dates or raisins, chopped	½ cup	125 ml
vegetable oil	3 tbsp.	45 ml
egg, slightly beaten	1 medium	1 medium
sugar	¼ cup	50 ml
buttermilk or low fat yogurt	1 cup	250 ml
whole wheat flour	1¼ cup	300 ml
baking soda	1 tsp.	5 ml
salt	½ tsp.	2 ml

1: Heat water in a mixing bowl for 1 min. on
   high heat. Stir in bran & set aside.
2: If using compressed dates, heat 30 sec.-1 min.
   on high heat to soften. If using raisins or
   whole dates, chop or process them.
3: Mix flour, soda & salt together. Set aside.
4: Beat oil, egg, sugar & buttermilk together.
   Stir in the bran mixture & dates or raisins.
5: Stir in flour mixture just until moistened.
   Let the batter sit for 5 minutes then bake:

   1 muffin   -   30-45 secs.
   2 muffins   -   50 sec.- 1 min. 10 sec.
   4 muffins   -   1½ - 2¼ min.
   6 muffins   -   2½ - 3½ min.

per muffin:

Dietary Fibre 6.8 g	Cholesterol 22 mg	Carbohydrate 33 g
Total Fat 6 g	Unsaturated Fat 4.6 g	Sodium 282 mg
Energy 180 kCal	Protein 5 g	Calcium 51 mg	Iron 2.4 mg

BREADS &
BREAKFASTS

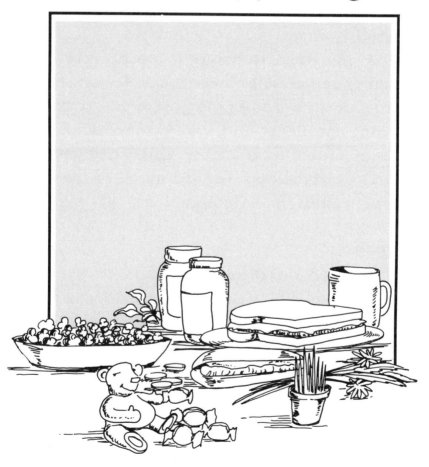

BREADS

WARMING:

Breads are very porous & reheat very quickly. Most people overdo bread & dry it out. You'll find you can warm 1 dinner roll in 10-15 seconds & ½ dozen in 30-45 seconds. It's best if they're wrapped in paper towel, napkin, or cloth napkin. This keeps them moist but not soggy.

RISING:

If you have 10 power levels on your oven, you can rise yeast breads beautifully! Power level 1, or 10% power, is just enough to activate the yeast without killing it. Put a glass of water in the oven with the loaf of bread & "microwave" for 20 minutes on power level 1... what a difference!!

BAKING:

You can bake yeast breads in the microwave oven ... but you'll find they won't "crust" & that's usually the best part! If you prefer the crust on your bread, you'll have to bake it conventionally.

It will take 4-6 minutes on high heat to bake 1 loaf of bread in the microwave oven.

HOBO BREAD

This sweet bread is wonderful with cheese....

raisins	1¾ cups	425 ml
water	¾ cup	175 ml
baking soda	1 tsp.	5 ml
whole wheat flour	2 cups	500 ml
salt	½ tsp.	2 ml
brown sugar	¼ cup	50 ml
egg, slightly beaten	1 medium	1 medium
vanilla	1 tsp.	5 ml

1: Combine raisins, water & baking soda in a casserole. Cook uncovered, 8-10 minutes on high heat.
2: Combine the flour, salt, sugar, egg & vanilla. Mix into the raisin mixture.
3: Line a loaf pan with wax paper & pour the bread mixture in. Let the batter sit for 5 minutes.
4: Bake 10 minutes on "half" power (Level 5 or medium), then for 2-3 minutes more on high heat if needed. Let stand 5 min.

per slice:

> Dietary Fibre 2.1 g Cholesterol 11 mg   Carbohydrate 25 g
> Total Fat 1 g Unsaturated Fat 0.4 g Sodium 75 mg
> Energy 107 kCal Protein   3 g Calcium 17 mg Iron 0.9 mg

* If your loaf pan bakes the bread unevenly, you can "shield" the ends from over cooking by using a piece of foil on each end. Allow a 1"(2.5cm) clearance between the foil & the oven's walls. Readjust if there is any arcing (sparks).

HOVIS BREAD

Remember Hovis Bread?... a wonderful healthy bread! This has no yeast or eggs & because most of the ingredients are dry, I measure up more than one loaf at a time & keep the extra in bags in the freezer. When I want a loaf of bread I just take a bag out of the freezer, add the 2-3 liquid ingredients & I have a loaf ready to bake! Remember to keep this in the fridge as it has no preservatives... & I like this "toasted"!

whole wheat flour	2 cups	500 ml
white flour	1 cup	250 ml
baking powder (See Tip P.98)	½ tsp.	2 ml
baking soda	½ tsp.	2 ml
salt, optional	1 tsp.	5 ml
brown sugar	3 tbsp.	50 ml
oatmeal	½ cup	125 ml
wheat germ	¼ cup	50 ml
bran	¼ cup	50 ml
sunflower seeds	¼ cup	50 ml
vegetable oil	¼ cup	50 ml
milk	1¾ cups	425 ml
molasses, optional	2 tbsp.	30 ml

1: Combine all the dry ingredients & mix with a fork or spoon.
2: Stir in the liquid ingredients & then let the dough sit for about 5 minutes, to allow the leavening agents to start

SOUR CREAM'S TWIN DESSERT DIP OR TOPPING P. 121

working.

3: Line a loaf pan (or bundt pan) with wax paper to allow for easy removal once baked.... remember, no need to grease pans in the microwave oven!

4: Place the dough in the lined pan & sprinkle with paprika for colour. Cover with vented plastic wrap.

5: Cook for 9 minutes on "half" power, (50%, level 5 or medium) then another 2-4 minutes on high heat.

per slice:

Dietary Fibre 2.5 g	*Cholesterol 0 mg*	*Carbohydrate 19 g*
Total Fat 4 g	*Unsaturated Fat 3.6 g*	*Sodium 24 mg*
Energy 126 kCal	*Protein 4 g*	*Calcium 38 mg Iron 1.0 mg*

Variations:

For an even healthier bread for all of you "cholesterol-conscious" cooks, add ½ cup (125ml) of oat bran in place of ½ cup (125ml) of the whole wheat flour.

If for dietary reasons you need to omit one of the dry ingredients, just replace it with an equal quantity of another dry ingredient.

Combine whole wheat flour with white flour when baking. (muffins turn out better using whole wheat flour!)

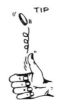

TIP

CORN BREAD

make this in an 8" (20cm) round pan & store in fridge to keep longer.

vegetable oil	¼ cup	50 ml
honey	¼ cup	50 ml
eggs	2 medium	2 medium
buttermilk	1 cup	250 ml
whole wheat flour	1 cup	250 ml
corn meal	⅔ cup	150 ml
baking powder (See TIP P.98)	1 tsp.	5 ml
baking soda	¼ tsp.	1 ml
green onions or chives, optional	¼ cup	50 ml
corn flakes, crushed or corn meal	} — Topping —	

1: Beat together oil, honey, eggs & milk.
2: Stir in dry ingredients. Let stand 5 min.
3: Pour into pan & sprinkle crushed corn flakes or cornmeal as a topping.... I also sprinkle with paprika for colour!
4: Bake 4-6 minutes on high heat or until a toothpick comes out clean.

per slice:

Dietary Fibre 1.0 g Cholesterol 22 mg   Carbohydrate 12 g
Total Fat 4 g Unsaturated Fat 3.0 g Sodium 41 mg
Energy 88 kCal Protein 2 g Calcium 20 mg Iron 0.5 mg

Variations:

CHILIES : can be used in place of (or as well as) green onion

LOW FAT GRATED CHEESE: is nice on this after it comes out of the oven.

ENGLISH MUFFINS

whole wheat flour	2 cups	500 ml
bran	½ cup	125 ml
sugar	2 tsp.	10 ml
salt	1 tsp.	5 ml
baking soda	⅛ tsp.	.5 ml
low fat milk	1 cup	250 ml
water	¼ cup	50 ml
active dry yeast	1 envelope	1 envelope
cornmeal	2 tbsp.	30 ml

1: Mix flour, bran, sugar, salt & baking soda in a mixing bowl.
2: Combine milk, water & yeast in a casserole & heat 1-1½ min. on high, just until warm (105°-115°F), stirring 2-3 times. Stir into the flour mixture.
3: Sprinkle half the cornmeal in the bottom of a microwave safe loaf pan.
4: Spoon the batter into the loaf pan & sprinkle with remaining cornmeal. Cover with vented plastic wrap.
5: Cook 30 sec. on half power (50%, level 5). Let stand 10 min. Repeat this step & the bread will double in volume.
6: Bake uncovered, 6-7 min. on high. Test with a toothpick & let stand 10 min. before turning out on a cooling rack.

per slice:

*Dietary Fibre 2.2 g Cholesterol 0 mg Carbohydrate 11 g
Total Fat 0 g Unsaturated Fat 0.3 g Sodium 122 mg
Energy 52 kCal Protein 2 g Calcium 22 mg Iron 0.7 mg*

* This freezes well & is best served toasted.

EGGS

Canada's Food Guide lists eggs as part of a balanced diet. They are high in protein & contain many nutrients essential for good health.

If you are someone who needs to watch your cholesterol intake, it is wise to limit the number of eggs you eat. The yolk of an egg is high in cholesterol. For this reason, you can replace the yolk of an egg in baking with an egg white.... (ie) if a recipe calls for 1 egg, use 2 egg whites instead, or use an egg substitute (See P.121).

SCRAMBLED EGGS

# of eggs	soft margarine	milk	cooking time
1	1 tsp. (5ml)	1 tbsp. (15ml)	45 sec- 1 min.
2	2 tsp. (10ml)	2 tbsp. (30ml)	1½-1¾ min.
4	4 tsp. (20ml)	4 tbsp. (60ml)	2½- 3 min.
6	6 tsp. (30ml)	6 tbsp. (90ml)	3½- 4¼ min.

1: Blend margarine, milk & eggs together. Add salt & pepper to taste.
2: Cook covered, on high heat, stirring 2-3 times.

* Eggs will look slightly moist ... but .... will finish cooking during standing time.

HARD BAKED EGGS

For salads or sandwiches .... no need to wrestle with peeling a hot egg!

Beat egg with a fork. For each egg, beat in 1 tbsp. (15ml) of low fat milk. Allow 1 min./egg on high heat in a covered casserole. The result will be a hard cooked "omelette".... now just chop & add to your salad or sandwiches.

HOT CHOCOLATE

cocoa	1 tsp.	5 ml
white sugar	2 tsp.	10 ml
lowfat milk	1 cup	250 ml

1: Combine cocoa & sugar in a mug. Blend with the back of a spoon.
2: Stir in milk ... don't worry ... the lumps <u>will</u> disappear!
3: Heat 1½ min./mug on high heat.

per cup:

*Dietary Fibre 1.1 g Cholesterol 4 mg   Carbohydrate 22 g
Total Fat 1 g Unsaturated Fat 0.4 g Sodium 128 mg
Energy 128 kCal Protein 9 g Calcium 311 mg Iron 0.4 mg*

Most commercial granola cereal is high in sugar & saturated fat. For good nutritional value, make your own. (See P. 120.)

OMELETTE

eggs	3 medium	3 medium
low fat milk	3 tbsp.	50 ml
pepper	1/8 tsp.	.5 ml
soft margarine	1 tbsp.	15 ml

1: Beat together the eggs, milk & pepper.
2: Melt margarine in a glass pie plate for 30-45 seconds on high heat.
3: Pour the egg mixture into the pie plate & cook covered, 1½-2 minutes on high heat.
4: Lift cooked edges to the centre with a spatula, allowing the uncooked center to flow to the outside edges. Cook covered another 1-1½ minutes on half power (50%, medium). Let stand 1-2 minutes "carry over cooking time". Now carefully fold your omelette in half, using a spatula.

per ½ recipe:

Dietary Fibre 0.0 g Cholesterol 330 mg Carbohydrate 2 g
Total Fat 13 g Unsaturated Fat 9.6 g Sodium 160 mg
Energy 175 kCal Protein 10 g Calcium 68 mg Iron 2.1 mg

VARIATION:

5: Sprinkle one or all of the following toppings on your omelette, after Step 4, reserving a small amount for a topping.

sautéed green pepper	- 1½- 2 min / ½ cup
sautéed mushrooms	- 1½- 2 min / ½ cup
sautéed onions	- 1½- 2 min / ½ cup
low fat cheddar cheese, grated	- to taste
chives & basil	- to taste

* You can sauté in the microwave oven without added fat... just make sure to cover the vegetables during cooking.

6: After adding your desired toppings to your omelette, carefully fold it in half using a spatula. Sprinkle the remaining toppings on top for a garnish. Let stand 1-2 minutes longer. Heat, covered with wax paper, another 30 seconds on high heat.

* Omelette for one?.... just cut the recipe & the time in half!

OATMEAL

No more pots to scrub...no more mess!

oatmeal or oat bran	⅓ cup	75 ml
water	⅔ cup	150ml

1: Combine oatmeal & water in a bowl & cook 1½-2 minutes on high heat.
2: Let stand 1 minute for "regular" & 3-4 minutes for "old fashioned".

* You will find the nutritional breakdown of oatmeal or oat bran on the box.

VARIATION: add chopped fruit &/or cinnamon.

CREAM OF WHEAT

| cream of wheat | 3 tbsp. | 50 ml |
| water | 1 cup | 250 ml. |

1: Cook as for "OATMEAL" (previous page). You will find the nutritional breakdown of Cream of Wheat on the box.

GRANOLA

Many commercial brands are high in fat. Make your own & store in an airtight container.

rolled oats	2 cups	500 ml
wheat flakes	½ cup	125 ml
oat bran	¼ cup	50 ml
wheat bran	¼ cup	50 ml
chopped almonds, or other nuts	¼ cup	50 ml
raw sunflower, or sesame seeds	¼ cup	50 ml
honey	¼ cup	50 ml
oil	¼ cup	50 ml
chopped fruit	½ cup	125 ml
(raisins, dates, dried fruit)		

1: Combine all ingredients, except fruit, in a large casserole. Cook uncovered, 6-8 min. On high heat, stirring 2-3 times.
2: Stir in fruit, cool, then store in an airtight container.

per ¼ cup serving:

Dietary Fibre 2.0   Cholesterol 0 mg   Carbohydrate 17 g
Total Fat 6 g   Unsaturated Fat 4.7   Sodium 8 mg
Energy 119 kCal   Protein 3 g   Calcium 16 mg   Iron 0.9 mg

EGG SUBSTITUTE

baking powder (see Tip p. 98)	½ tsp.	2 ml
flour	2 tbsp.	30 ml
water	2 tbsp.	30 ml
vegetable oil	½ tbsp.	7 ml

1: Mix all ingredients together & add to recipes in place of 1 egg.

per recipe:

Dietary Fibre 0.5 g Cholesterol 0 mg   Carbohydrate 12 g
Total Fat 7 g Unsaturated Fat 5.9 g Sodium 133 mg
Energy 115 kCal Protein   2 g Calcium 13 mg Iron 0.4 mg

SOUR CREAM'S TWIN

A "low fat twin" to the real thing!

low fat cottage cheese	1 cup	250 ml
lemon juice	1 tbsp.	15 ml
skim milk	2 tbsp.	30 ml

1: Place all ingredients in a blender or processor.
2: Beat until smooth & creamy.

per tbsp:

Dietary Fibre 0.0 Cholesterol 1 mg   Carbohydrate 0 g
Total Fat 0 g Unsaturated Fat 0.0 Sodium 53 mg
Energy 10 kCal Protein 2 g Calcium 10 mg Iron 0.0 mg

VARIATIONS:

Vegetable dip : add 1-2 tsp (5-10 ml) dill weed
   & 1-2 tsp (5-10 ml) minced onion

salad dressing : make "vegetable dip" & dilute with milk if too thick

dessert topping: serve with honey if needed or puréed fruit. See Photo p. 112a

YOGURT CHEESE

"Little miss Muffet sat on a tuffet....."

    make your own yogurt cheese to re place cream cheese in recipes. Place low fat yogurt in a cheescloth-lined colander. Set the colander over a casserole & place in the fridge overnight. The liquid (whey) will drain off into the casserole & leave the solid cheese (curd).

QUARK CHEESE

    Alias "Bakers Cheese"... is low in fat, creamier than cottage cheese & can tolerate higher temperatures than yogurt. Use as a substitute for cream cheese or sour cream in your recipes.

TIP

Heat your grapefruit in the morning 30-45 secs. on high heat.

Avoid saturated fats (those that are hard at room temperature). (ie) coconut & palm oil

"Buttermilk" actually has no butter in it & very little fat!

INDEX

QUILCHENA
CONSULTING LIMITED

Quilchena Consulting Ltd. (QCL) provides computer software and processing services for the nutrient analysis of food intakes for individuals or groups, the nutrient analysis of recipes and menus, and other food and nutrition related applications. The QCL software has an extensive database of foods, nutrients and allergens that are based on Canadian values. Processing services are available for individuals, professionals (physicians, dietitians, nutritionists and educators), and institutions (hospitals, long–term care, schools and colleges) via fax, mail and modem for fast response.

Please check for information on the following:

      [ ]   all of QCL's products and services
      [ ]   processing services for nutrient analysis
      [ ]   nutrient analysis software
      [ ]   foodservice management software

Name:_____

Address:_____

            _____

            _____

Telephone:_____ Fax:_____

Complete your address and forward this page to:

Quilchena Consulting Ltd.
305 Viaduct Avenue West
Victoria, B.C
V8X 3X1 Canada
Tel (604) 380–1588 Fax (604) 385–4761

FOR ADDITIONAL COPIES OF SUSAN CALDER'S
MICROWAVE COOKBOOKS, SEND CHEQUE OR
MONEY ORDER TO:

SUSAN CALDER
1534 SHORNCLIFFE HEIGHTS
VICTORIA, B.C.
V8P 5R6

- - - - - - - - - - - - - - - - - -

PLEASE SEND ME:

__COPIES OF "WELCOME TO MICROWAVE COOKING"
($14.95/copy)

__COPIES OF "WELCOME TO MICROWAVE LIVING"
($14.95/copy)

__COPIES OF "WELCOME TO A HEALTHY ALTERNATIVE"
($10.95/copy)

* PLUS GST & $2.00 SHIPPING & HANDLING/BOOK

* PRICES SUBJECT TO CHANGE

* ORDER 5 BOOKS ...... GET 1 FREE

NAME:_____

ADDRESS:_____

CITY:_____PROVINCE:_____

POSTAL CODE:_____

(U.S. ORDERS PAYABLE IN U.S. FUNDS)